Euripides

Andromache
Hecuba
Trojan Women

Euripides

Andromache
Hecuba
Trojan Women

Translated by Diane Arnson Svarlien
Introduction and Notes by Ruth Scodel

Hackett Publishing Company, Inc.
Indianapolis/Cambridge

19 18 17 16 15   2 3 4 5 6 7 8

For further information, please address:

Hackett Publishing Company, Inc.
P.O. Box 44937
Indianapolis, IN 46244-0937

www.hackettpublishing.com

For information regarding performance rights, please email us at
Permissions@hackettpublishing.com

Cover design by Brian Rak
Text design by Meera Dash
Map by William Nelson
Composition by William Hartman

Library of Congress Cataloging-in-Publication Data

Euripides.
    [Selections. English. 2012]
    Andromache, Hecuba, Trojan women / Euripides ;
translated by Diane Arnson Svarlien ; introduction and
notes by Ruth Scodel.
        p. cm.
    Includes bibliographical references.
    ISBN 978-1-60384-735-3 (pbk.) —
    ISBN 978-1-60384-736-0 (cloth)
    1. Euripides—Translations into English. I. Arnson Svarlien,
Diane, 1960– II. Scodel, Ruth. III. Title.
PA3975.A2 2012
882'.01—dc23
                                                    2011043973

Contents

Introduction

Classical Athenian tragedy combined elements of different Greek performing arts to appeal to the eye with costume and dance, to the ear with song and speech, and to the mind and memory with new versions of familiar tales, new twists on old narrative patterns, and new presentations of recurrent ethical, religious, and political dilemmas. Greek festivals of the archaic and classical periods could include highly dramatic performances by rhapsodes, professional reciters of poetry (especially of Homer). Many festivals also included performances of the various kinds of choral song: choruses of men, of young women, and of boys. Both rhapsodic and choral performances included passages of direct speech (in Homer, extensive ones), which facilitated the invention of drama. A tragedy featured masked and costumed actors who presented a dramatized version of a (usually legendary) story in spoken verse, and also a chorus, again masked and costumed, that represented a group appropriate to the story being presented. The chorus would sing and dance in response to the dramatic action. Tragedies did not have to be "tragic" in the modern sense—a tragedy could have a happy ending—but they were serious, and their poetry was in a grand style. The main characters were usually ancient royalty, and their misfortunes or dangers were beyond those likely to happen to most people. Watching a tragedy was a powerful experience: the costumes were splendid, the singing and dancing were expressive, and the noble language carried viewers away. Often the audience, knowing the basic outline of the story, would anticipate the disastrous outcomes of the characters' decisions and feel intense suspense and sympathy as the characters blundered. Audiences often wept (but sometimes hooted if they did not like the play). Tragedy required both an emotional and an intellectual response from the spectator. Characters suffered and lamented, but they also argued, and the plots and choral songs invited the spectator to think about why events could have happened this way.

The City Dionysia and Euripides

Tragedies were performed exclusively in competitive settings. For the most important festival, the City Dionysia, a public official, the archon, selected the three tragedians for each year's competition. A wealthy private individual paid for the expenses of each chorus while the city paid the actors directly. Each competitor presented three tragedies and a satyr-play, a humorous work that always employed a chorus of satyrs, the half-human, half-horse followers of Dionysus. Judges voted on the first, second, and third prizes for each poet (and so for the whole set of four plays each had composed), and later for the lead actor as well. A complicated judging system introduced an element of chance into the outcome: although ten judges voted, five votes were randomly selected, and if one production had a majority at that point, it won; if not, two more votes were drawn, and if there was still no majority, one vote at a time was added.[1] Although the competition was very real, being accepted as one of the three competitors (known as having been "granted a chorus") was probably the most significant part of the process. Euripides, the youngest of the three tragedians whose work is partially extant, rarely won first prize, but he clearly received choruses regularly and was evidently very much admired.

The performances at the Dionysia also included five comedies and lyric "circular choruses" of both men and boys from each of the ten divisions of the Athenian citizen body. Evidently, the Athenian audience had stamina, and it was a large audience, perhaps as many as fifteen thousand, the largest regular gathering the city had. The theater could hold more people than the Pnyx, where the assembly met. Tragedy was evidently popular. By the latter part of the fifth century BCE, tragedy had been added to the program at the less important festival of the Lenaea; this setting probably offered a chance for a tragedian to prove himself before receiving a chorus for the Dionysia. Local festivals also included tragedies, though these were usually repeat performances of successful plays from the Lenaea or Dionysia.

---

1. This reconstruction is from C. W. Marshall and S. van Willigenburg, "Judging Athenian Dramatic Competitions," *Journal of Hellenic Studies* 124 (2004): 90–107. The article also analyzes statistically how often the procedure gave the "wrong" result.

The tragedian's first job was to make his material new. Although history and mythology provided the basic stories, the dramatists had great freedom within those stories. They usually worked with a single episode from the vast cycles of legend. Choosing a particular event, the tragedian imagined how it might have come about. He then created characters who fit the plot he had in mind, selecting and configuring traditional stories of their pasts and futures around this moment. For example, in Homer's *Odyssey,* Hermione, daughter of Helen of Troy and Menelaus, married Neoptolemus, son of Achilles. The death of Neoptolemus at Delphi was also traditional and could be told in varying versions with more or less sympathy for Neoptolemus. Andromache was probably already depicted as the concubine of Neoptolemus and the mother of his children before Euripides' plays. We do not know who first told the story that made Orestes the second husband of Hermione. Sophocles wrote a *Hermione* (only fragments have survived) that probably told of her being first promised to Orestes by her grandfather but then pledged by her father to Neoptolemus. It was Euripides, however, who brought all these strands together and created the Andromache, Hermione, Menelaus, and Orestes of *Andromache.* It was a traditional part of the story of the Trojan War that a Greek, either Neoptolemus or Odysseus, killed Hector's son Astyanax (Scamandrius), though this story was probably open to variation; at a later period, at least two cities in the Troad, the region around Troy, claimed Astyanax as a founder. Euripides in *Trojan Women* has them commit this murder not during the sack of Troy but afterward, as a policy decision, in cold blood. Euripides typically exploits any possibilities the old stories provide for showing corrupt political decisions.

Composition and Date

The three plays in this volume, all set in the aftermath of the Trojan War and showing the fates of the women of the royal family of Troy, come from roughly the same period of Euripides' career. The production of the last, *Trojan Women,* is firmly dated to 415 BCE. The others can be approximately dated by Euripides' metrical practice, which became steadily bolder through the approximately thirty-three–year period when he created his extant plays.

Andromache did not appear in the records of the Athenian festival productions and must have been first produced in either a local festival in Attica or another city. Metrically, it belongs around 425, and *Hecuba* dates from slightly later. Both plays were written and produced during the first part of the Peloponnesian War, in which Athens and its subordinate allies fought Sparta and its allies. This first war, the "Archidamian War," lasted from 431 to 421 and was followed by a period of cold war before full-scale hostilities erupted again in 413. *Trojan Women* belongs to this intermediate period; it must have been written before the Athenians massacred the men of Melos and enslaved the Melian women and children in 415, but late enough that the likely outcome was known—and the massacre had taken place by the time the play was performed. Similarly, although the Athenians had not yet invaded Sicily when the tragedy was in preparation, they had debated and planned this imperialist adventure.

The Plays

Although the three plays in this volume include many of the same characters and events, they were not composed as a group and are fully independent of each other. Hecuba was always the wife and then widow of Priam and the mother of Hector and other children, but her character could be very different in different plays. The Hecuba of *Hecuba,* who exploits Agamemnon's sexual relationship with her daughter as if it were a marriage, is not exactly the Hecuba of *Trojan Women,* who finds Cassandra's joyous acceptance of her situation incomprehensible. The Menelaus of *Andromache* is not exactly the same character as in *Trojan Women,* and Andromache's description of her marriage to Hector is different in the two plays: in both she describes herself as a perfect wife, but in *Andromache* she stresses her complete acquiescence in her husband's extramarital affairs (235–39),[2] while in *Trojan Women* she speaks of knowing when she should have her own way and when she should yield to her husband. The plays are linked only because the poet avoided repeating himself: *Trojan Women* passes very quickly over the killing of Polyxena, probably because Euripides had treated it at length in *Hecuba.*

By the time he composed *Andromache,* Euripides had been producing tragedies for thirty years. Of his extant plays, *Alcestis,*

---

2. In this Introduction, all line references to plays in this volume are to Arnson Svarlien's translation.

Medea, Hippolytus, and *Heraclidae (Children of Heracles)* are older than *Andromache,* the first three of these being among his most admired works. As a tragedian Euripides was a complete master of his craft. It is important to bear this in mind, because all three dramas presented in this volume can seem odd to the modern eye. *Trojan Women* can appear more a pageant of misery than a drama. The other two have, in the eyes of some critics, too much plot; *Hecuba* presents two stories about the aftermath of Troy's fall, while *Andromache* shifts its focus from the title character to her enemy, Hermione, and introduces an entirely new set of dramatic tensions halfway through.[3] Yet *Hippolytus,* one of Euripides' most esteemed works, though its plot is tightly unified, presents a similar shift in focus. In the first part of the play, Phaedra is the center of the audience's sympathy. After she falsely accuses Hippolytus and kills herself, he becomes the focus and the audience must pity him.

Euripidean plots often include such shifts of focus and sympathy and unexpected arrivals that change a play's direction. In *Heracles,* for example, the hero rescues his family and seems to have achieved a happy ending halfway through when Madness appears and makes him murder his wife and children. These jolts are often the point of Euripidean drama. His world is not without inner logic, but it is not predictable, because everything that happens on the stage is only a part of a larger set of events. Euripides also often juxtaposes extreme pathos with dry rationality, forcing the audience to both feel intensely and think about the implications of the dramatic action.

Following Euripides' usual practice, each play in this volume includes at least one debate, or *agôn. Andromache,* indeed, has three: one between Hermione and Andromache, one between Andromache and Menelaus, and another between Menelaus and Peleus. *Hecuba* presents a trial of Hecuba before Agamemnon (and two other scenes that could be considered *agônes*), and *Trojan Women* includes a trial of Helen, judged by Menelaus. In all these scenes, the audience's sympathies are strongly on one side from the start—even those who are appalled by Hecuba's revenge in *Hecuba*

---

3. Both of these once controversial plays have received an important and sympathetic treatment: for *Hecuba,* Judith Mossman, *Wild Justice: A Study of Euripides'* Hecuba (Oxford: Oxford University Press, 1995); for *Andromache,* William Allan, *The* Andromache *and Euripidean Tragedy* (Oxford: Oxford University Press, 2000).

have little sympathy for Polymestor—and the arguments are unlikely to change them. The debates, however, give the other side a chance to argue and force the characters to explain themselves.

All three of these dramas present women who have experienced the most profound loss warfare could inflict. The men in their families have been killed, their city has been destroyed, and they themselves have been enslaved. They suffer not only grief for their families but utter deracination and a sudden and profound loss of social status. Such was the possible outcome of defeat in war, but Greeks did not usually go to this extreme in warfare against each other, although the Athenians enslaved the survivors in an attack at Chaeronea, in Boeotia, in 447 BCE. In 427, however, the Athenians, after they defeated their rebellious ally Mytilene, voted to execute the male population but changed their minds the next day. Even Thucydides, whose *History of the Peloponnesian War* presents a debate on the issue in which both speakers carefully avoid emotional or moral arguments, calls such action "savage" (3.36.4). The Athenians' Spartan opponents in 427 killed every man in Plataea who could not say that he had helped the Spartans during the war, then they enslaved the few remaining women—most of them had been sent with the children and elderly to safety in Athens. Only later, in 418, did the Athenians kill the men of Torone and Scione; the massacre of the Melians took place in 415. So Euripides' initial interest in the aftermath of such warfare was not prompted by any recent atrocity that his own city had committed. *Andromache,* indeed, expresses a profound loathing for Sparta that the audience is clearly intended to share, and Delphi and its god Apollo, who favored Sparta during the war, also appear in a very negative light (Apollo does not come off well in other Euripidean plays, either— especially *Electra*).

Trojans in Greek tragedy are a complicated group. Following the Persian invasion of Greece in 480–479, the Trojan War clearly became the mythical precedent and analogue for the Greco-Persian War. In this paradigm, Trojans represent everything that is un-Greek. This way of seeing Trojans is active in *Andromache,* where Hermione expresses contempt for Andromache's foreignness, and in *Trojan Women,* where Andromache accuses the Greeks of acting like stereotypical non-Greeks—that is, impiously and cruelly. *Hecuba,* too, stresses the Greek–barbarian divide. Yet Homer, whose epics were the basis of Athenian education, had already made the Trojans sympathetic and not profoundly different from their Greek enemies.

In *Andromache,* Andromache's "barbarian" values were probably no more distant from those of the Athenians in the audience than Hermione's Spartan ones. In *Hecuba,* Trojans are contrasted not only with Greeks but with the Thracian king Polymestor.

Andromache

Andromache assumes the audience has some familiarity with its mythological background. Peleus married the sea goddess Thetis (there were various versions of why and how this took place) and they had a son, Achilles. However, Thetis returned to her elderly father in the sea; Homer never explains why she left Peleus (later, Apollonius of Rhodes says that Peleus interrupted her attempt to make Achilles immortal, and she left in anger [*Argonautica* 4.866–79]). Seeking to keep Achilles from joining the Trojan expedition, Thetis hid him on Scyros among the daughters of King Lycomedes. He seduced one of them, Deidamia, and she gave birth to a son, Neoptolemus. After Achilles' death at Troy, Neoptolemus joined the Greek fighters there and was among the leaders in Troy's capture. As a prize he was awarded Andromache, the widow of Troy's greatest fighter Hector, whom Achilles had killed. In some versions of the story, Neoptolemus himself killed Hector's and Andromache's son.

The play is set in northern Greece, in Phthia in Thessaly, near Pharsalus. The action begins at the shrine of Thetis, with a palace represented by the stage building (the town is some distance away). Euripides' plays always begin with a prologue that clarifies the particular version of the story that is relevant for the play. In this case, Andromache tells how she saw her husband Hector killed and her son Astyanax thrown from the towers of Troy (but not, apparently, by Neoptolemus). She was then brought back to Phthia (where Neoptolemus lives, although his grandfather Peleus continues to reign) as Neoptolemus' concubine and bore him a son. Neoptolemus then married Hermione, the daughter of Helen of Troy and King Menelaus of Sparta, but the marriage has not been happy or fertile. Although Andromache says that her sexual relationship with Neoptolemus is over, Hermione believes that Andromache has used magic to make her infertile and unattractive to her husband. Neoptolemus has traveled to Delphi to apologize for his earlier complaint against Apollo for killing Achilles (this second journey, and its motive, are probably Euripides' invention). In his absence,

Hermione's father Menelaus has come from Sparta to help her dispose of her rival. Andromache, fearing for her life, has sent her son away to an unidentified home where she hopes he will be sheltered, while she herself has taken refuge at the shrine of Thetis.

Tragedians often exploited a license to set their works in a world whose social norms were ambiguous. The rules are not exactly the same as either those of the present or those known from Homer, whose epics took place in the long-ago heroic age in which the events shown in tragedies were believed to have happened. In Homer, we hear of concubines and their sons—though Laertes, Odysseus' father, is said never to have had sexual relations with Eurycleia, Odysseus' nurse, in order to avoid his wife's anger (Odyssey 1.433). Concubines' sons are fully part of the household and along with the sons of a legitimate wife inherit property, although they have lower status. In contemporary Athens, by contrast, the son of a slave could never be a citizen or inherit his father's property. Andromache says that Hermione accuses her of wanting to usurp Hermione's place in the household, which would also be impossible in the world of the audience. Peleus' tirade against Menelaus, however, includes an attack on the Spartan custom of having girls exercise in public, as they did in Euripides' own time. Hermione's opening speech (152–87) emphasizes both that she is Spartan (Athenians tended to see Spartans as arrogant bullies) and that she comes from a rich family, which assimilates her to the contemporary stereotype of the woman who feels superior to her husband because of her family's wealth. Andromache makes the very contemporary argument that even if her children were Neoptolemus' only sons, public opinion would never let them rule in Phthia.

The play begins very much as a domestic melodrama. Greeks certainly believed that women might use magic against each other, and they would expect a wife to be intensely jealous of a concubine in the house. (Men were not expected to be faithful, but they were expected to show respect for their wives by not having other sexual partners in the house.) Hermione, however, blames Andromache for what cannot be her fault, as if she had chosen to be Neoptolemus' concubine. Menelaus is an outright villain who persuades Andromache to leave her sanctuary at the shrine by making her choose between her own life and that of her son—and then, when she consents to die for her son's sake, announces that Hermione will kill the child anyway. Although Andromache's ideals of wifely subservience go beyond what Greeks would expect of their wives and give her a distinctly foreign tone, in her helplessness and devotion to her child she is the sympathetic character. The Chorus of local women simply confirm this sympathy—when the women arrive (122 ff.) saying that they have been afraid lest Hermione find out that they feel for Andromache, they prepare the audience to despise Hermione before she speaks a word.

As the drama unfolds, *Andromache* at first seems to be an exciting but not especially profound play. The spectator spends the first part of the play wondering whether Neoptolemus will return in time, since he seems to be the only hope. The servant has gone to seek help from Peleus, but the dialogue leads the audience to believe that he will not respond, since he has failed to do so in the past. So Peleus' appearance (at 557) is a surprise, and so is Menelaus' cowardice. It is a characteristic Euripidean twist that Andromache's rescue comes unexpectedly, but that it also seems to bring the drama to a premature end. The Chorus sing in praise of Peleus, appropriately ending this segment—but the play cannot be over yet.

The plot then takes an entirely new turn beginning at 870: now Hermione is terrified of her husband's anger, and Orestes, son of Menelaus' brother Agamemnon, pops up to rescue *her*. An entirely new back story about Menelaus' promise to marry Hermione to Orestes is revealed. While Andromache had sent a messenger to Peleus, so that his entry, though surprising, was prepared, Orestes has not been mentioned at all.

The first shift is a change of focus. The first part of the play is entirely Andromache's story. The other characters can almost be seen as necessary pieces in a game: Loyal Slave, Jealous Wife, Treacherous Spartan, Rescuer. Suddenly, though, while a spectator may or may not feel pity for Hermione, we cannot help but see her as a character who has her own story, and she becomes the focal character. Hermione's fear is a direct consequence of what has happened so far, so although we have not left the plot with which the drama started, the perspective now is certainly different. Whether or not we are at all convinced by her claim that other women aggravated her jealousy and drove her to try to murder Andromache, she is no longer simply The Opponent.

A few minutes later, Orestes tells his story (900 ff.), and, like Hermione, he has a justified grievance that has led him to an act of excessive revenge. Then the messenger narrates events at Delphi (1106 ff.)—where Neoptolemus, we learn, has been murdered—and the story of Neoptolemus becomes the center of attention.

The murder of Neoptolemus has nothing to do with Hermione's hatred of Andromache; Orestes' love for Hermione is the only link between Neoptolemus' death and the rest of the plot. The narrative of Neoptolemus' murder, in which it appears that Apollo intervenes to kill a man who is trying to make amends, introduces a whole new theme into the play—for the first time, we are invited to wonder about the role of the gods. Then the death of Neoptolemus makes the grieving Peleus now matter for himself, and not just as the savior of Andromache.

When Thetis appears at the very end of the play (1278), she not only announces what is to happen, but presents one last turn of the kaleidoscope. Andromache is to move to Epirus, where her son will become ruler of Molossia and founder of a dynasty. So Troy and the family of Peleus, both apparently eradicated, will continue, and a larger history subsumes the local events of the play. Peleus will be immortalized, and Achilles too has a blessed afterlife.

The effect and significance of the tragedy lie largely in this repeated shifting. The play first offers its audience a simple but suspenseful plot in which an innocent victim is threatened. After she is saved, however, the plot opens and expands, so that the audience sees not just the story of one character, but the interlocking stories of them all. It is not a conventionally well-made play, in which each event is the consequence of what has gone before, and yet the entire story, when we see it as a whole, makes sense. Neoptolemus, who never appears alive, seems to have made a whole series of forgivable but fatal errors: he insulted the god Apollo; he insisted on marrying Hermione despite Orestes' claim, and he was arrogant to Orestes; he kept his concubine Andromache in his house when he married Hermione, even though he stopped having relations with her. All these mistakes have disastrous consequences. Instead of presenting them in order and making a cautionary tale, however, the play puts Neoptolemus on the margin and offers a series of surprising turns.

Hecuba

Hecuba, unlike Andromache, has a single focal character, but the tragedy shows two distinct actions. Through line 680, the play centers around Hecuba's daughter Polyxena, and for the rest of the play, her revenge for the murder of her son Polydorus. The prologue, spoken by the ghost of the murdered Polydorus, introduces both, but the play keeps them distinct until the end, when both victims

are buried together. Only after Polyxena is dead does Hecuba find
her son's body and realize that Polymestor, the Thracian king to
whom Priam had entrusted Polydorus for safekeeping during the
Trojan War, must have murdered him for the gold that was sent
along with him as a trust. The play is organized around the contrast
between Hecuba's inability to influence the outcome of the first
plot and her skill at persuading Agamemnon to allow her to take
revenge and at luring Polymestor into her trap. In the first half, she
is helpless, but in the second, she is ruthlessly efficient.

Modern readers and audiences are likely to be appalled by
Hecuba's vengeance and the grim satisfaction she finds in it. The
modern ethical tradition, especially Christianity, preaches against
revenge, although popular culture frequently endorses it. When
revenge means the killing of innocent children, for us the deed has
nothing to do with justice. However, the ancient Greeks' traditional
ethical code was based on the principles of reciprocity and retaliation: an admirable man helped his friends and harmed his enemies.
The code was not beyond question, and Socrates would deny it
completely, but it was the governing cultural rule. The Greeks also
were much likelier than we are to accept that an entire family could
suffer for the wrongs of one of its members.

Frequently in tragedy, the gods punish relatively small offenses
against themselves in horrific ways—for example, in *Hippolytus,*
because Hippolytus has refused to worship her, Aphrodite destroys
not only Hippolytus himself but Phaedra, who has not offended her
at all. Such excess is evidently troubling; Greeks believed in revenge,
but they also believed that it should be proportional to the wrong
done. In *Hecuba,* Polymestor's crime would have seemed as bad to
Greeks as it does to us, perhaps even worse, since Priam trusted him
as a friend. If a god inflicted Polymestor's sufferings, they would be
unambiguously just. He deserves to be childless because he has murdered another's child, and his greed to find the hidden gold of Troy,
whose hiding place Hecuba had promised to show him in order to
lure him into an ambush, is appropriately punished by blindness.
The gods seem indeed to be implicated in Hecuba's revenge, since
it is only possible because the winds delay the Greeks' departure
(934–36) and change as soon as the plan is complete (1350).

Similarly, Hecuba understands what has happened to Polydorus
because she had a dream, and a meaningful dream implies divine
intervention. Still, even Greeks would probably not have listened
complacently as Polymestor narrated how the women first dandled

his little boys and then murdered them. It is entirely possible that
Polymestor deserves his fate and that the gods enable Hecuba to
take her revenge, even though the revenge is destructive to the soul
of Hecuba herself. Polymestor (1325 ff.) announces that Hecuba
will become a dog with burning eyes, after whom the promontory
called Cynossema ("dog's marker") will be named: dogs in Greek
can symbolize both shamelessness and fierce protectiveness, and
nothing tells the audience which is more important here. In any
case, Polymestor is a character whose foolish arrogance is typical
of tragedy: he evidently never imagined that Hecuba could have
learned what he has done or that she would take revenge. Whether
we find Hecuba's vengeance satisfying or horrifying, it demonstrates
the power of the weak.

The two halves of the play echo each other. In both, positive
reciprocity (gratitude) is at stake. Odysseus claims that the Greeks
must repay Achilles with the honor his ghost demands, because such
recompense motivates men to fight. Yet Euripides adapts the story
Helen tells in the *Odyssey* (*Odyssey* 4.235–64, *Hecuba* 238–49)
of how she recognized Odysseus when he came as a spy to Troy so
that Odysseus' life depended on Hecuba. Odysseus acknowledges
that Hecuba saved him, but he does not accept her argument that
he should save Polyxena in return. For Odysseus, gratitude matters
in public, because it has large-scale political effects, but he ignores
its obligations in private. In the second half of *Hecuba*, Agamemnon
agrees to allow Hecuba's vengeance at least in part because she
appeals to the feelings created by his sexual relationship with her
daughter Cassandra, as if it were a marriage (863–73). This is also
a kind of gratitude, *charis,* even though he has taken Cassandra by
force and she and her family had no choice. Agamemnon does not
take revenge himself on Hecuba's behalf because he is afraid of the
popular response—he may be willing to regard Hecuba almost as a
member of his family, but he is afraid to be seen to do so (885–893).
The Greek leaders are politicians, and they consistently make their
decisions for political reasons.

The deaths of Hecuba's children are set in careful contrast to
each other. One victim is a girl, killed before a large crowd in a
ritual; the other, a boy, is murdered secretly and his corpse thrown
into the Hellespont in the hope that it will vanish. Polyxena,
because her killing is ritualized, has the chance to die nobly and
win respect; Polydorus has no such opportunity. Instead, the hidden murder, perpetrated for gold, is avenged behind the cover of

the *skênê* (stage building), where, thanks to Hecuba's persuasion, Polymestor believes that Priam's gold is concealed.

Greeks of the classical period did not practice human sacrifice but seem to have felt a horrified fascination with it. It is peculiarly horrible here that the Greeks debate whether to perform the sacrifice. Like human beings everywhere, Greeks distinguished allowable from forbidden violence. Almost everything that took place during the sacking of a city was allowed, unless it happened at a spot sacred to a god. Killing women who had survived was not accepted practice. In *Hecuba* the Greeks perform the sacrifice although they are not threatened by imminent destruction and see no other way to appease a god. Odysseus' decisive support for the sacrifice is entirely based on his calculation that the life of a slave has less value than the honor of a dead warrior (128–33). Apart from Agamemnon and Odysseus, the only speakers explicitly mentioned who favor the sacrifice are the two sons of Theseus—the Athenians.

Euripides repeatedly returned to the theme of the voluntary sacrifice of a young and noble victim: this was the main theme of his lost *Erechtheus,* and he shows self-sacrifice in *Heraclidae (Children of Heracles), Phoenician Women,* and *Iphigenia at Aulis.* In most of these, the victim's decision is truly free, and the situation is truly desperate; the decision to be sacrificed to save the community is a more extreme case of every soldier's commitment to risk death for the community. Polyxena is a special case, because she does not benefit those she loves by her decision to die. Indeed, she chooses only not to resist the inevitable. (Iphigenia's situation in *Iphigenia at Aulis* is similar.) But she still engages in a typically Euripidean speech of meticulous analysis of her situation, arguing that death is preferable to a life in slavery (352–92). Talthybius narrates not only how she offers herself to the sword, but how her behavior prompts spontaneous demonstrations of admiration from the Greek army (569–606). Polyxena's clarity of purpose and the Greeks' response to it give the episode a dignity to counteract its horror—a dignity that would be appropriate for the end of a play. The Chorus at 676–79 sing of the grief of a young woman in faraway Sparta and of a mother of dead children; the expression of shared loss again seems to mark dramatic closure.

Although the ghost of Polydorus announces in the prologue that his body will be found so that his mother can bury him, the second half of the play is a shock. When Hecuba realizes what has happened, she begins thinking about revenge immediately. This vengefulness is not inconsistent with her character in the earlier part of the play, since the situation is different: against the victorious Greeks she has no chance of effective resistance, but against Polymestor, a third party, she might. Hecuba is a mother above all, and if she cannot protect her daughter, she will mourn her; but if she has not been able to protect her son and has a chance at revenge, she will take it. Nonetheless, the change in Hecuba is sudden and absolute. Hecuba becomes a skilled manipulator in persuading Agamemnon: she tricks Polymestor as if she were a practiced con artist, and neither Hecuba nor the other women hesitate to engage in gruesome violence. As in *Andromache,* with Hermione's sudden transformation from swaggering aggression to panic after her father leaves, Hecuba's change of direction shows Euripides' fascination with how people's behavior depends on their situations as much as on their characters. His tragedies are full of people whose extreme circumstances drive them to actions they would never have imagined. This is one reason his war plays, especially, remain relevant—we ourselves know only too well that war and its aftermath can prompt violence and cruelty that their perpetrators would never have performed under normal conditions.

Trojan Women

In 415 Euripides produced three tragedies presenting episodes from the Trojan War. Although only *Trojan Women* survives, we have considerable fragments of *Alexandros,* and we know a little about what happened in *Palamedes*. The central character of *Alexandros* is Alexander (Paris), whose mother, while pregnant, dreamed he would destroy his city; she exposed him (left him to die) as a baby, but he survived. As an adult he was recognized by his family—though only after they planned to murder this stranger who defeated all the Trojan princes at his own funeral games. In *Palamedes,* which took place during the war, Odysseus schemed against Palamedes, his enemy and rival. Odysseus, not wanting to join the Trojan expedition, had pretended to be mad; Palamedes, as ingenious as Odysseus, exposed him. In the play, Odysseus successfully framed Palamedes for allegedly planning to betray the Greeks to Priam, and Palamedes' brother Oeax managed to tell Palamedes' father Nauplius what had happened.

Both of these episodes resonate in *Trojan Women*. In the prologue, Athena and Poseidon plan to punish the Greeks for their impiety during the sack of Troy by causing a great storm; this is the only prologue of an extant Greek tragedy that predicts events that will happen after the play is over. According to the traditional story, during this storm Nauplius created a misleading beacon that caused many shipwrecks, an event probably foreshadowed in *Palamedes*. In *Trojan Women*, Helen, debating with Hecuba, blames Hecuba for the war, since she gave birth to Paris. The loose trilogy of *Alexandros, Palamedes,* and *Trojan Women* showed the prelude to the war on the Trojan side, the political corruption on the Greek side, and the devastation of the war's aftermath for both. In the first play, Cassandra predicts the fall of Troy; in *Trojan Women*, she predicts the death of Agamemnon, the Greek leader (364–70). In the first play, ashamed at losing in Paris' funeral games, the Trojan prince Deiphobus plots Paris' murder; in the second, Odysseus successfully conspires against Palamedes; in the third, the entire Greek army decides to murder a small child. The guilt becomes deeper and wider.

Although Hecuba is the center of *Trojan Women*, present throughout the play, she is in large part a means for the audience to see the experience of the other women. Because she is old, she has value to the Greeks only as a symbol of Troy's defeat. Hecuba and the women of the Chorus can simply grieve. What will happen to them in slavery is completely out of their control. Cassandra, Andromache, and Helen, however, have futures to be negotiated. They are valuable not only as high-ranking women but sexually, and because they are sexually desirable they may have something to trade. Similarly, in the first part of *Hecuba*, Hecuba herself is powerless. She can beg Odysseus, but it is Polyxena who genuinely makes a decision—to die willingly. The first part of *Hecuba* could almost be another episode in *Trojan Women*. Most of the play's action lies in Hecuba's interactions with these three women, and these encounters make the play more than a parade of the miseries of war, although the songs of the Chorus and Hecuba's laments and speeches convey the terrible contrasts between Troy's past—blessed by the gods—and its present: between the four women's lives then and now.

The first important event of the play is Talthybius' arrival to collect Cassandra (245), but it is Cassandra's entry at 314 that provides the initial Euripidean shock. The captive women of the Chorus have sung a lament and expressed their anxiety about where they will be carried as slaves when Talthybius, the Greeks' herald,

enters to report that Agamemnon has selected Cassandra. When
he sees torches blazing inside, he suspects that the Trojan women
have chosen to burn themselves alive instead of accepting slavery,
but Hecuba immediately knows that Cassandra must be carrying
the torches. And when Cassandra enters, carrying them, it immediately becomes clear that she is happy. Her elderly father and her
remaining brothers have all died. Her city is destroyed. Before the
fall of Troy, Cassandra was a princess; now she is a slave. She was
a virgin, but one of the Greek leaders, Ajax son of Oïleus, raped her
in the temple of Athena where she had taken refuge. An Athenian
girl had no voice in selecting her husband and was usually married very young, which must have been terrifying; but marriage
brought her a social role that she recognized as appropriate. She
would have the expectation that children would give her purpose
and prestige, and she had the protection of her natal family if her
husband mistreated her. Yet Cassandra is celebrating Agamemnon's
desire for her and his decision to have her as a slave concubine as
if it were a wedding, although she is unlikely to have any of the
goods of marriage. The audience, of course, knows the story, as
does the prophet Cassandra: Agamemnon's wife Clytemnestra will
kill both Agamemnon and Cassandra as soon as he reaches home.
That would hardly seem to be a reason to rejoice, yet Cassandra is
not only celebrating herself but wants Hecuba to celebrate with her.
In a style typical of Greek tragedy, Cassandra first sings, so that her
emotions come fully to the audience first, and then speaks, explaining why she feels what she feels: because Clytemnestra will resent
Agamemnon's arrival with a concubine and be even more power-
fully motivated to kill him, Cassandra will avenge Troy (368–70).
She then delivers a dizzyingly paradoxical speech in Euripides' most
brilliant rhetorical style, demonstrating that the Trojans are more
fortunate than the Greeks.

In the second episode, Andromache enters with her infant son
Astyanax (591), on a wagon, on her way to the ships of Neoptolemus.
She directly confronts her decision: she can either retain all her
loyalty to Hector, or she can allow herself to feel affection for her
new husband (and she calls him that). Whether or not they had seen
Andromache, the original audience would have known that her
son by Neoptolemus was the ancestor of the Molossian kings, so
they knew in general what the outcome would be. The play avoids
reminding the audience that Neoptolemus is the son of Achilles,
who killed Hector, which could make her choice to accept him

seem disgusting. Hecuba follows traditional Greek moral teachings in encouraging Andromache to give in to her fate and try to create a future for herself and for her son. No sooner has she given this advice, however, than Talthybius enters (736) to announce that the Greeks, at the urging of Odysseus, have decided to throw the boy from the walls of Troy. Neoptolemus is not his killer, as he was in some versions; the story makes Andromache as honorable as possible but the Greek army as a whole utterly contemptible. At the end of the episode, Andromache faces the same dilemma, but its terms have profoundly changed.

Then Menelaus enters (879), announcing that he will take Helen home and then kill her. The ensuing *agôn* is a debate for Helen's life. Helen does not win the argument, in the view of either Menelaus or the audience. Even if she is partially right and the war is not entirely her fault, a character who completely denies any responsibility for her actions is unlikely to convince. Yet neither Hecuba nor the Chorus seem confident that Helen will be punished, and the tradition, going back at least to the *Odyssey,* has her living comfortably with Menelaus in Sparta after she reaches home. Clearly, Helen is saved not because she is persuasive, but because Menelaus cannot resist her.

Although the debate really ends the dramatic action—there are no further decisions or conflicts—the funeral of Astyanax, and the final burning of the ruins of Troy, remain. The audience would expect Andromache to perform this rite herself, so Euripides carefully has Talthybius explain why Neoptolemus has hastened home, taking Andromache with him. Talthybius reports that Andromache asked that the child be buried on Hector's shield. Hecuba's speech over the child (1278 ff.) is a bitter attack on the Greeks, and the presence of the shield allows her to speak about Hector as well. The funeral and the subsequent burning of the city together represent the final annihilation of Troy: the boy was its final hope for the future, and the city itself disappears.

Trojan Women presents the appalling aftermath of war, but it is not really an antiwar play. Both Cassandra and Hecuba insist on the nobility and valor of the Trojans. War, for Greeks, seemed often to be an inescapable evil, and they could not imagine that it would ever vanish. Like many other Greek treatments of the Trojan War, the play suggests that Helen was not worth so much suffering, and it also looks at the proper limits of violence. The "message" of *Trojan Women* is the most consistent message of Greek tragedy—that human fortunes change, that nothing can be assumed to be permanent. Once Troy enjoyed divine favor, beautifully evoked in choral song, but now the city is being destroyed forever.

This awareness of fragility is the basis of tragic morality. Mortals need to be aware that the misfortunes of another could come upon themselves and must show restraint accordingly. The Greeks, who have already offended the gods when the play begins, murder Astyanax; they fear the possibility that the boy will be dangerous when he grows up, but not divine retaliation for their impiety during the sack of Troy. Agamemnon takes Cassandra and has no idea that Clytemnestra is waiting to murder him. While the play honors military valor and does not endorse pacifism, it discourages warfare for its own sake and the excessive cruelty that so often accompanies it. Athena and Poseidon, who turn against the Greeks in the prologue, were the special protectors of Athens itself. In the context of the war's recent atrocities and the Sicilian expedition, the play implies that war should be undertaken only for great cause, and with an awareness of how it leads people to forget their mortal limits.

Politics and Power

The atrocities of war in both *Hecuba* and *Trojan Women* do not take place amid the frenzy of battle; these are deliberate political decisions made in the aftermath of war. Some suffering in war is inevitable, but the treatment of Hector's death in *Trojan Women* is gentle: his mother is obviously to some extent consoled by the memory of his courage and strength. The sacrifice of Polyxena and the murder of Astyanax are not inevitable and are decided by assemblies. They are not motivated by revenge, either. It might be more tolerable to see Astyanax killed because soldiers whose friends were killed by Hector could not bear the thought that Hector's line would survive. The decision, though, seems to be pragmatic; Hecuba assumes that they are afraid that some remnant of the Trojans could someday unite under his leadership.

One of the worst dangers of warfare, then, seems to threaten only the victors. The aftermath of war is a field in which the worst aspects of political maneuvering have free play, since the defeated cannot resist. The Athenian debate over Mytilene and the Spartans' treatment of the Plataeans in the Peloponnesian War are especially relevant to Euripides' thought, because they were such vivid examples of the cruelty of victors' decisions. The Athenians had to decide whether it would be better to make an example of the Mytileneans in order to deter their other allies from rebelling, or to be merciful so that rebels in the future would not assume that they might as well fight to the last man, since they would be massacred anyway.

All three plays are about situations in which the disparity of power is immense. Hermione and Menelaus have power; Andromache has none. They abuse her because they can. The Greek army is willing to oblige the ghost of Achilles by sacrificing a Trojan princess, since they have one available and it is not a serious cost to them. Polymestor assumes that he can safely murder Polydorus and keep the gold, since nobody will have the power or inclination to seek justice. The Greeks decide to kill Hector's little son because it is better to be safe, and they see no risk—nobody will avenge him.

For Euripides, unconstrained power makes people likely to forget their human limits, and victory in war creates such a situation of power, but not because fighters are carried away in battle, or because the violence in which they have engaged overwhelms them—at any rate, Euripidean characters do not say, for example, that after so many killings one more does not matter. Instead, they calculate, and then conclude that killing will be advantageous. Odysseus is an important character in both *Hecuba* and *Trojan Women,* even though he never appears on stage in the latter, because he is the master calculator and persuader, and the aftermath of war puts him in control. In *Andromache* the main difference between the domestic tyranny of Menelaus and Hermione and the assemblies at Troy would seem to be that Hermione actually hates Andromache and believes that Andromache is doing her harm, whereas the Greeks in *Hecuba* and *Trojan Women* are simply indifferent to the suffering of others.

In *Andromache,* the gods at the end want in some fashion to reconcile Greeks and Trojans and to ensure that neither side vanishes completely. Andromache's son promises a new history. The other two plays offer no such hint of redemption.

RUTH SCODEL

Translator's Preface

The Texts

These translations draw on the work of many scholars; they do not follow any single editor's Greek text. My primary texts of reference have been Diggle's Oxford Classical Text editions (vols. 1–2), and I have kept Kovacs' Loeb editions (vols. 2 and 4) always at my elbow, along with the commentaries of Stevens and Lloyd (*Andromache*), Gregory, Collard, and Tierney (*Hecuba*), and Lee and Barlow (*Trojan Women*). Professor Luigi Battezzato kindly let me see a partial draft of his forthcoming Cambridge University Press commentary on *Hecuba,* which was another invaluable resource. For more information on textual issues, see the Endnotes and Comments on the Text (with headnote on p. 177); for full references to works mentioned in this Translator's Preface, see the "Editions, Commentaries, and Textual Discussions" section of the Suggestions for Further Reading.

The line numbers in the margins of this book are those of my English versions; the line numbers of the corresponding Greek text appear in brackets at the top of each page. In the Preface and Endnotes, line numbers designated AS refer to my translations.

The Language

My continuing aim in translation is fidelity: I have tried to create contemporary English-language approximations of what Euripides' plays are in Greek. Since the plays in Greek are brilliantly crafted, stage-worthy works of poetry, nearly every line presents a humbling challenge and the need to orchestrate the clamor of competing loyalties. Throughout, I have been attentive to the basic semantic content and the meter of each verse, and tried to capture the tone and register of each speaker. Beyond that, different aspects of Euripides' poetic art come to the fore at different times. Many passages are strongly flavored with assonance and alliteration, and it is worth the effort to try to capture this effect in some way. For example, at *Hecuba* 1214–15 of the Greek text I have represented Euripides' heavy repetition of the vowel *eta* with two long *a* sounds followed by a string of *o* sounds (1266–68 AS). Euripides' play of sounds extends even to near-anagramming of words, as at *Hecuba* 156–57 Greek (148 AS). Sometimes word order is a significant feature: a climactic word or name might be thrown into enjambment, as Helen's name is at *Trojan Women* 34 AS (35 Greek). At other times it might be important that a character is using a word that is rare and poetic (see, e.g., *Andromache,* endnote xx), or a phrase with a colloquial flavor, or language drawn from the contemporary Athenian world of politics, law, or philosophy. Often it is important to preserve the figurative language that characters use, to reflect a play's patterns of imagery: for example, ships and sailing, both literal and metaphorical, are prominent in *Trojan Women* (on this and other images, see Barlow [1986], p. 32 and passim).

Verse translation resists systematic handling and demands case-by-case negotiations; nevertheless, I have tried to be systematic in my translations of Euripides' repeated words and phrases, continuing the approach I described in the Translator's Preface to *Alcestis, Medea, Hippolytus:* "That is, if I repeat an English word, there is a pretty good chance that it reflects a repetition in the Greek, and readers can expect that I have followed any repetitions in the Greek that are thematically significant" (Arnson Svarlien [2007], p. xxxiv). For example, forms of the Greek word *eremos* occur in all three plays in this volume (most often in *Andromache*), and I have consistently translated them with forms of the word "deserted." Forms of *anankê* appear in all three plays and are especially prominent in *Hecuba,* and I have used "compulsion" and "compel" to translate them. Consistent translation enables readers to follow Euripides' echoes; in *Hecuba,* for example, when the blinded Polymestor sings his monody, he uses language that was used earlier in the play by Hecuba and Polyxena: "accursed" and the verb "hack" (1100, 1123 AS) recall Hecuba's denunciation of Polymestor in the anguished song she sings after she realizes what he has done (744–47 AS), and the phrase "this outrage, this insult" (1118 AS) echoes Polyxena (207–8 AS).

I have tried to translate consistently even when the thematic significance of a word is not obvious. The word "hand" occurs oddly often in *Hecuba* (forty times!), and I have retained this feature, keeping the word in lines where it might otherwise have seemed dispensable, such as 548–49 AS (527–28 Greek). Some words are thematically important but cannot be adequately translated by a single English word in all cases; see, for example, *Hecuba,* endnote xi on *charis,* which I usually translate as "favor" or "gratitude" but

have also translated as "grace/gracious," "reward," and "delight."
My goal has been to give readers a sense of the texture of Euripides'
language, by reflecting his lexicon as much as possible without
adhering too rigidly to a set of word-for-word equivalents. For
keeping track of the language, Allen and Italie's *Concordance to
Euripides* (1954, with *Supplement* by Collard [1971]) has been an
essential tool.

The Meters

Euripides wrote his plays in highly formal verse whose effects range
from natural-sounding conversation in the dialogues to artfully
patterned mosaics of sound, sense, and image in the choral odes.
Many elements of the original performances of these plays are all
but lost to us: music and choreography; costumes, masks, and sets;
the sound of the actors' voices. What remains in the texts is the
poetry. These plays, like all classical Athenian tragedies, were written entirely in poetic form; the closest Euripides comes to prose is
the occasional brief interjection, such as "Aah!" Aside from these,
every line is composed following some type of regular rhythmic
pattern. Different meters (patterns of heavy and light syllables) were
traditional for different parts of each play.

In English, meter is based on patterns of stressed and unstressed
syllables. Ancient Greek verse, on the other hand, was quantita-
tive, based on patterns of long and short syllables; for example, a
syllable with the vowel sound "o" as in "hop" was short, and one
with "o" as in "hope" was long. Despite this difference in the basis
of the English and ancient Greek systems, the patterns themselves—
iambic, trochaic, anapestic, dactylic—are comparable, and so it is
possible to get some sense of Greek meters through their English
analogues. In these translations I have used different English verse
rhythms to reflect the changes in meter in the Greek originals.

1. Spoken Dialogue

Iambic Trimeter   The regular meter for speech in Athenian tragedy was the iambic trimeter. An iamb, in Greek and in English, is
a short syllable followed by a long syllable (or unstressed followed
by stressed); for example, the word "toDAY" is an iamb. Although
the Greek iambic line consists of six iambs, it is called a trimeter
because it was treated as three units of two iambs each:

x-LONG-short-LONG—x-LONG-short-LONG—x-LONG-short-LONG

In the "x" (anceps) positions, a long could be substituted for a short. Aristotle said that iambic rhythm was native to everyday Greek speech, and in ordinary conversation people will unintentionally produce lines of iambic verse (*Poetics* 1449a; cf. *Rhetoric* 1408b). The same is true of contemporary English; like ancient Greek, it naturally falls into patterns of alternating light and heavy syllables. An NBC Evening News broadcast on March 8, 2011, reported on popular anger "directed at the nation's capital"—the phrase is a perfect iambic pentameter.

The English iambic pentameter is the meter I have used wherever Euripides uses iambic trimeter. As the name suggests, it is a line made of five iambs: da-DUM da-DUM da-DUM da-DUM da-DUM. Many variations are traditionally allowed—unstressed syllables can be added to, or subtracted from, most positions—and I have taken advantage of this liberty. An example of a line that follows the regular five-iamb pattern is the second line of *Andromache:* "the place I came from once upon a time."

Trochaic Tetrameter   According to Aristotle, trochaic tetrameter was the original spoken meter of Athenian tragedy; the switch to iambic trimeter made tragic dialogue more dignified and natural-sounding (*Poetics* 1449a; cf. *Rhetoric* 1404a). Aeschylus uses trochaic tetrameter extensively in the *Persians,* and briefly at the end of *Agamemnon.* Sophocles makes very little use of this meter; Euripides evidently revived it in the latter stage of his career, and he uses it in all of his surviving later plays (for an overview, see Drew-Bear [1968]). In this volume, trochaic tetrameter is spoken by Cassandra in one brief passage of *Trojan Women* (466–84 AS, 444–61 Greek).

A trochee is a backwards iamb, a long (or stressed) syllable followed by a short (unstressed) syllable, like the word "TABle." Like iambs in Greek drama, trochees are used in units of two each, and four such units make up a tetrameter. However, the trochaic tetrameter line is catalectic; that is, the final syllable is missing, so the line has this rhythm:

table tabl*e*—table tabl*e*—table tabl*e*—table chair

Like the iambic trimeter, this meter also allows anceps syllables, which can be either short or long; these are represented by the italicized "*e*"s in the diagram above. In *Trojan Women* I have translated

Cassandra's trochaic tetrameters following the Greek pattern, for example, "Emblems of my frenzy for the god I love, farewell, farewell!" (474 AS).

2. Anapests

I have used anapestic rhythms wherever Euripides does. An anapest is short-short-LONG, like the word "vioLIN." Anapestic rhythms are used throughout Greek tragedy; they are often used by the Chorus for their own exits and entrances, or to announce the approach of another character. For example, the Chorus in *Andromache* direct the audience's attention to an arriving party with "Here's our lord coming back / from the Delphian land" (1213–14 AS). Anapests can also be used for passages in a higher emotional register than ordinary speech, or to make a transition between speaking and singing. They are either chanted (marching anapests) or sung (lyric anapests), with slightly different rules defining the two types (for a summary of the differences, see Gregory [1999], p. 51, and Lee [1976], p. 80). In both *Hecuba* and *Trojan Women,* Hecuba's first words are chanted anapests that lead into sung anapests.

3. Lyric Meters (Songs)

Euripides' plays featured a great deal of singing, in a variety of meters. Songs were normally accompanied by the aulos, a double-reed wind instrument with a sound similar to the oboe. The lyric meters have the highest emotional coloring and stand at the greatest distance from ordinary speech. Unlike iambs, trochees, and anapests, most lyric meters do not translate readily into familiar English equivalents. Each of Euripides' songs is a unique creation metrically, based on traditional groups of rhythmic patterns.

Songs with Strophic Response   The most formal lyric passages are the choral odes, which were danced as well as sung. These are organized into pairs of stanzas called strophe and antistrophe, occasionally followed by a third stanza with a different rhythm called an epode. Any stanza in the text identified with one of these names was set to music and sung.

Strophes and antistrophes always match each other metrically, and the rhythmic repetition was probably emphasized in the choral odes by melodic phrases and dance movements that repeated or mirrored each other. This feature, called response, is the one metrical attribute of Euripides' lyrics that I have consistently attempted to reproduce. For example, the first line of the strophe of the ode that begins at *Hecuba* 462 AS, "Breeze, ocean breeze," is matched rhythmically by the first line of the antistrophe, "Salt-sweeping oar" (472 AS).

The strophe/antistrophe structure was not limited to choral odes; for example, Hecuba sings duets in strophic responsion with Polyxena in *Hecuba* (146–209 AS), and with the Chorus in *Trojan Women* (164–209 AS). In *Andromache,* mother and child sing a duet in which Menelaus' chanted anapests intervene between the corresponding strophe and antistrophe (517–49 AS). In *Trojan Women,* Cassandra sings a monody with strophic responsion (316–47).

Songs that do not have stanzaic form are indicated by stage directions. In some cases, where singing is interspersed with speaking, I have italicized the sung passages.

Dochmiacs   Dochmiacs are a type of lyric meter used to express intense excitement, fear, or agitation. Euripides uses them, for example, in lyric dialogues between an agitated singer and a calmer speaker (*Andromache* 842–82 AS, *Hecuba* 706–47 AS, *Trojan Women* 1274–99 AS), in a brief choral song mixed with iambic trimeters (*Hecuba* 1053–67 AS), and in Polymestor's extended monody after he is blinded (*Hecuba* 1090–1149 AS). There were many variations on the dochmiac, whose basic rhythm was short-LONG-LONG-short-LONG. As with the choral lyric meters, I have not tried to reproduce dochmiacs syllable for syllable, but I have tried to capture their flavor, and I have observed responsion wherever it is found in the texts.

4. Elegiac Couplets and Dactylic Hexameter

Andromache includes the only passage of elegiac couplets in extant Greek tragedy, Andromache's lament at 108–21 AS (103–16 Greek). Elegiac meter was often accompanied by the aulos and was associated with a variety of topics and genres, including mournful songs. An elegiac couplet consists of a line of dactylic hexameter (the meter of epic), followed by a shorter line that is traditionally called a pentameter.

The dactylic hexameter contains six feet; each foot is either a dactyl (LONG-short-short: a backwards anapest) or a spondee (LONG-LONG). The sixth foot of each line is always a spondee, and the fifth is usually a dactyl, so most lines end with the rhythm LONG-short-short LONG-LONG, "shave and a haircut."

The pentameter line is not really five dactylic feet; rather it is 2.5 + 2.5 feet. The pattern LONG-short-short—LONG-short-short—LONG, two dactyls plus a long syllable, is called a hemiepes. Two hemiepes, with a word boundary between them, make up the so-called pentameter line: "LIons and TIgers and BEARS—LIons and TIgers and BEARS." In the first hemiepes, a long syllable can be substituted for two shorts. Here is a couplet that follows the regular pattern, with only one optional spondee (the second foot) in the hexameter line:

> It was for her, O Troy, that the Greeks came and took you at
> spearpoint,
> burning my city: the swift war god a thousand ships strong . . .
> (*Andromache* 110–11 AS)

After Andromache's elegiac lament, the Chorus begin their ode in dactylic hexameter, as if to continue Andromache's song. Appropriately for material so closely connected with the Trojan War and heroic epic, all three plays in this volume contain dactylic hexameters: see also *Hecuba* 76–77, 88–89 AS (73–75, 90–91 Greek), and *Trojan Women* 618–29 AS (595–606 Greek). I have translated Euripides' elegiac couplets and dactylic hexameters into English analogues of these meters.

Acknowledgments

I am grateful for all the support I have had in writing these translations. I have relied on the accomplishments of the editors, commentators, and scholars listed in the Suggestions for Further Reading, who have laid the scholarly foundations of my work. A Literature Fellowship from the National Endowment for the Arts enabled me to finish this project in 2010–11, and a semester of administrative leave from Georgetown College enabled me to translate *Andromache* in 2008. In the summer of that year, Charles Martin offered an insightful critique of *Andromache* at the Sewanee Writers' Conference. These translations have also been improved by useful comments and suggestions from Ruth Scodel (to whom I am grateful as well for the valuable Introduction and footnotes in this volume), John Svarlien, and Hackett's anonymous readers. Aaron Svarlien helpfully read and commented on the plays, representing an important target audience: college students. Luigi Battezzato was very generous and forthcoming in sharing his work prepublication and in discussing individual passages in *Hecuba*. Working with Hackett Publishing Company is a great pleasure; I thank the entire staff, especially the unfailingly judicious and conscientious editor Brian Rak and managing editor Meera Dash.

My understanding of Euripides has been deepened by reading his plays with students over the years, most recently in my spring 2010 Ancient Drama class at Georgetown College, in which *Andromache* made its classroom debut. Seeing the plays on stage has been illuminating, too: Patrick Wang's 2008 Stella Adler Studio Conservatory production of my *Medea* translation was exciting proof that metrical translation can come alive in the theater, and Amy R. Cohen's 2010 Randolph College production of *Hecuba,* translated by Jay Kardan and Laura-Gray Street, helped me visualize the play and experience its emotional impact while I was working on it. My thanks go to these directors and their excellent casts, and to all my students, past, present, and future. Last but not least, thanks for essential support to the librarians of Centre College, the Claremont Colleges, Georgetown College, Lexington Public Library, Stanford University, and the University of Kentucky. For valuable help in the nick of time, thanks to David Kovacs and to Jennifer K. Nelson, librarian of the Robbins Collection at the University of California, Berkeley, School of Law.

This book is dedicated, with love and thanks, to John, Aaron, and Corinna Svarlien.

DIANE ARNSON SVARLIEN

ART WORKS.
arts.gov

Greece, the Islands, and the Troad

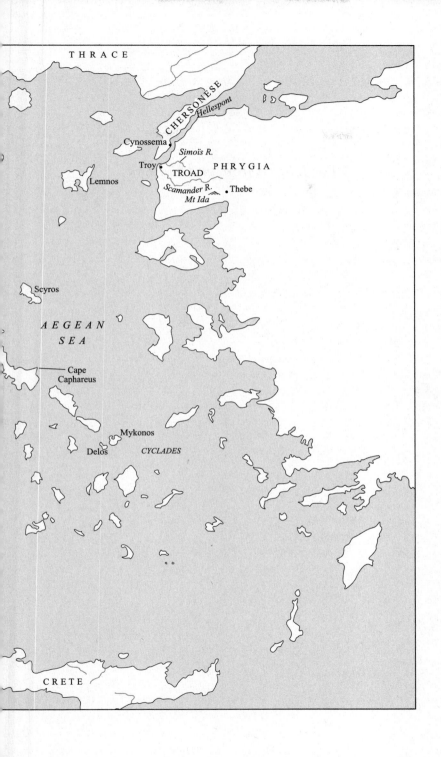

THRACE

CHERSONESE

Hellespont

Cynossema

Simoïs R.

Troy

PHRYGIA

TROAD

Lemnos

Scamander R.
Mt Ida

Thebe

Scyros

*AEGEAN
SEA*

Cape
Caphareus

Mykonos

Delos   *CYCLADES*

CRETE

For John, Aaron, and Corinna

Andromache

Andromache: Cast of Characters

ANDROMACHE	widow of Hector of Troy, now concubine of Neoptolemus
FEMALE SERVANT	formerly of Andromache, now of Neoptolemus' household
CHORUS	women of Phthia
HERMIONE	daughter of Menelaus of Sparta; wife of Neoptolemus
MENELAUS	brother of Agamemnon; co-leader of Greek attack on Troy
CHILD	of Andromache and Neoptolemus
PELEUS	father of Achilles; grandfather of Neoptolemus
NURSE	of Hermione
ORESTES	son of Agamemnon of Mycenae; nephew of Menelaus
MESSENGER	attendant of Neoptolemus
THETIS	sea goddess, daughter of Nereus, absent wife of Peleus, mother of Achilles

The exact date of *Andromache* is not known, and the play may not have had its first production in Athens. On metrical grounds it belongs about 425 BCE.

Andromache

SCENE: *At the shrine of Thetis, in Phthia near the city*
of Pharsalus in Thessaly. The stage building
represents Neoptolemus' house. Andromache
stays close to the altar and statue of Thetis a
little distance in front of the house. One side
entrance leads to Pharsalia (the area surround-
ing Pharsalus) and other parts of Thessaly; the
other leads to the road south, to Delphi and the
Peloponnese.

ANDROMACHE:
Oh my Asia, and my city, Thebe,
the place I came from once upon a time,
a bride arrayed with golden gifts, arriving
at Priam's royal hearth to be the wife
of Hector, and the mother of his child.[1]   5
Admired and envied then, Andromache
is now the most unfortunate of women.[i]
I saw Achilles kill my husband Hector;
I saw our child Astyanax thrown down
from the high city walls, the day the Greeks had taken   10
the Trojan plain.[2] The family I came from
was free and prosperous, but I arrived
in Greece as a slave, a spear-prize, a choice item
from the plunder of Troy, for Neoptolemus
the islander. I live here in the plains   15
of Phthia, bordering Pharsalia,

---

1. According to Homer's *Iliad,* Andromache, wife of Hector, was the
daughter of Eëtion, king of Thebe. This Thebe has been identified with a
Bronze Age site southwest of Troy, but it is not mentioned in Greek legend
except as the city of Eëtion and Andromache, destroyed by Achilles. The
wedding of Hector and Andromache is the subject of a poem by Sappho
(fr. 44).
2. In some versions, Neoptolemus, Achilles' son, killed Astyanax, but
Euripides avoids this detail.

where Thetis, a sea dweller, made her home
with Peleus; she shunned society
and lived apart from men. The people here
20 in Thessaly call this place "Thetideion"
in honor of that marriage with a goddess.
The household of Achilles' son is here—
in Pharsalia, he lets Peleus hold power.
He didn't want to take the scepter while
25 the old man was still living.[3] To this household
I have borne a male child, having lain
with Achilles' son, my master. It used to be
that in spite of all my troubles, I had hope
of finding some protection, just as long
30 as my child survived. But since my master married
Hermione the Spartan,[4] pushing me
off to one side—who wants a slave's bed!—
she torments me with insults and abuse.
She says that I use esoteric drugs
35 to make her childless, hated by her husband,
and that I want to force him from her bed
and occupy this house instead of her.
Not that I ever wanted my position—
and now I've left it, anyway. Great Zeus,
40 know this: I slept with him unwillingly.
But she does not believe me, and she wants
to kill me, and her father's helping her:
Menelaus has arrived from Sparta
for just this purpose; he's at the house already.
45 I'm terrified. I've come to take my seat
at Thetis' shrine, adjacent to the house,

---

3. Peleus, Achilles' father, married the sea goddess Thetis, but in most versions the marriage was not entirely successful, and Thetis returned to the sea. The unusual setting, away from the city, allows the machinations of Hermione and Menelaus to proceed without interference, and the detail that Neoptolemus did not claim power in Peleus' lifetime makes Neoptolemus sympathetic.

4. Hermione's mother is Helen of Troy. The play was composed during the Peloponnesian War between Athens and its allies and the Spartan-led Peloponnesian League, and both Hermione and Menelaus reflect anti-Spartan stereotypes.

to see if it will shelter me from death.[5]
This place is revered by Peleus
and his descendants, since it represents
his marriage to a Nereid, a goddess.[6]   50
I've sent away my only child in secret
to another house. I'm frightened for his life.
His father isn't by my side to help
his child; he counts for nothing at the moment.
He's left for Delphi, gone to make amends   55
to Loxias for the madness that possessed him
last time he went to Pytho: he asked Phoebus,
his father's killer, to make amends to *him*.[7]
He wants to see if asking for forgiveness
will win the god's good favor from now on.   60

(Enter a female Servant from the house.)

SERVANT:
My mistress—I don't hesitate to use
the title that you had in your own house
when we lived at home, on the Trojan plain;
there I cared for you, and for your husband
while he was alive. Now, I have some news—   65
I'm frightened one of the masters will find out,
but I pity you—Menelaus has plans,
terrible plans, for you and for your child.
You have to watch out.

---

5. Shrines were inviolable; it was sacrilege to drag a suppliant away from holy ground or to commit violence there.

6. A Nereid is one of the fifty daughters of the sea god Nereus.

7. Loxias and Phoebus are both names of Apollo; Pytho is another name for Delphi. The god Apollo helped Paris kill Achilles. According to the usual story, Neoptolemus went to Apollo's oracle at Delphi to demand justice from Apollo for Achilles' death and was killed there. There was a hero shrine of Neoptolemus near Apollo's temple ("heroes" were dead men who were believed to have supernatural powers near their tombs). Euripides has invented this second visit, preserving the traditional story while creating a more sympathetic Neoptolemus.

ANDROMACHE:

                    Dearest fellow servant—
70   once I was your lady; now I am
        unfortunate, a slave along with you—
        what do they have in mind? What strategies
        are they weaving this time? I know they want me dead,
        pathetic as I am.

SERVANT:

                    They want to kill
75   your child, poor woman. The one you sent away.

ANDROMACHE:

        Oh no. They found out that he's gone?[ii] But how?
        Poor me. I am destroyed.

SERVANT:

                  I don't know how,
        but I have learned from them that Menelaus
        is after him. He's left the house already.

ANDROMACHE:

80   Yes, I am destroyed. My baby, those two
        vultures will kill you, while your so-called father
        takes his time in Delphi!

SERVANT:

                  If he were here
        you would be better off. You've been deserted.

ANDROMACHE:

        And no word came that Peleus would be here?

SERVANT:

85   He's an old man, even if he comes.

ANDROMACHE:

        And yet I've sent for him—more than just once.

SERVANT:
What makes you think the messengers respect you?

ANDROMACHE:
Good point—why should they? . . . Can *you* take my message?

SERVANT:
Well . . . what excuse can I give for going out?

ANDROMACHE:
You'll find some strategy. You are a woman. 90

SERVANT:
It isn't safe. Hermione's on guard.

ANDROMACHE:
You see? When things look bad, you let your friends down.

SERVANT:
No, not at all! Don't say that! I will go;
since after all, no one has any regard
for a slave woman's life, or cares if I get hurt.[8] 95

ANDROMACHE:
Go, then.

(Exit Servant.)

    As for me, I'll stretch my voice
up to the sky in groans and lamentations
as I lie in my bed of tears. It's woman's nature
to take delight in having on our lips
and on our tongues the troubles that beset us. 100
And I have more than one cause for my weeping:
my native city and the death of Hector,
the brutal fate in which the gods entwined me
the day that I fell into slavery—
an undeserved misfortune. Never call 105

---

8. Andromache's readiness to manipulate her former slave is probably meant to seem excusable because she is a mother trying to save her child.

a mortal prosperous before you see
the state he's in when he goes down to death.

(Andromache sings in elegiac meter.)[9]

Paris brought back to the sheer heights of Troy no bride for
          his bedroom
  when he led Helen home; no, he brought madness and ruin.
It was for her, O Troy, that the Greeks came and took you
110   at spearpoint,
  burning my city: the swift war god a thousand ships strong,
taking my husband too—my Hector was dragged past the
          ramparts,
  lashed to the chariot rail of sea-dwelling Thetis's son.
Led from my own bedroom, I was brought to the edge of
          the seashore,
115   wrapping myself in my grief, servitude thrown like a veil
over my head, and my tears fell in streams; I was leaving
          behind my
  city, my bedroom, my poor husband, a corpse in the dust.
Oh, my misery. Why should I look on the sun any longer
since I'm Hermione's slave? Worn down by her, I have come
120 here to the goddess's altar, throwing my arms round her image,
  melting in tears, like a spring trickling down a rock face.

(Enter the Chorus.)

CHORUS:

[Strophe 1]

Friend, it has been a long time since you've taken your seat
          here at Thetis'
shrine; you will not leave it.

---

9. This passage (108–21) presents the only elegiac couplets in surviving tragedy. This meter is used in archaic Greek for poetry for the symposium with erotic, political, and moral themes. However, at least after around 415 BCE, the noun *elegos* is used to mean "lament," and some scholars have thought that Andromache's song is based on a Peloponnesian tradition of laments in this meter. This theory continues to be debated. Because the first line of an elegiac couplet is a dactylic hexameter, the meter of epic, Andromache's song is innovative while having a Homeric ring.

I am a woman of Phthia; nevertheless, I approach you—
you, who were born in Asia—   125
hoping to help you somehow
find some relief, a cure for the struggles that bind you
in hateful conflict with Hermione,
sharing a man, poor woman, a husband with two beds:
the child of Achilles.   130

[Antistrophe 1]

Realize just where you stand: be aware of your present
          misfortune.
Spartans are your masters;
you are a daughter of Troy. Will *you* fight with *them*?
          You should leave here
now, leave this sacrificial
altar, the sea goddess' home.   135
How does it help to ruin your body with weeping?
You're under their compulsion; you will find
they will use force. Why toil when your toil is useless
since you count for nothing?

[Strophe 2]

Come now, and leave this glorious shrine, the Nereid's
          quarters.   140
Realize you are a stranger,
a slave, a captive, held in a foreign city;
you are the most unfortunate of women
and your loved ones are nowhere to be seen here,
poor woman, sorrowful bride.   145

[Antistrophe 2]

Pitiful woman of Troy, when you came to the house of
          my masters
I felt compassion—and still do—
for you, but fear is holding me back; I'm keeping
quiet, despite my pity; I'm afraid that
Hermione, the child of Zeus's daughter,[10]   150
will see how I wish you well.

---

10. Helen, Hermione's mother, was the daughter of Zeus.

*(Enter Hermione from the house. She gestures to call
attention to her sumptuous clothing and jewelry.)*

HERMIONE:
    These fine things, this gold circlet that arrays
    my head, these robes with their embroidery
    were not bestowed upon me by the household
155   of Peleus or Achilles; no, I come here
    wrapped in gifts from my father Menelaus,
    from Laconia, from Sparta—a huge dowry.[11]
    And therefore I can say whatever I please.[iii]
    But you—a slave, a spear-captive—intend
160   to cast me out and occupy this house;
    you've made my husband hate me with your drugs
    and caused my empty womb to waste away.
    A woman from the continent is clever
    at things like that. But I will make you stop.
165   The Nereid's house, this altar and this temple,
    won't help you: you will die. And even if
    some mortal or some god intends to save you
    you'll be brought low. You must dismiss all thought
    of just how prosperous you used to be.
170   You'll fall down at my knee and sweep my floor,
    sprinkling Acheloüs' river water[12]
    from golden vessels, and you'll realize
    what land you're in. There is no Hector here,
    no gold for you, no Priam. This is Greece.
175   Poor thing, you really do have no more sense—
    you have the nerve to sleep with that man's son—
    his father killed your husband!—and to bear
    children to your family's murderers.
    This is the way barbarians behave:
180   father sleeps with daughter, son with mother,
    girl with brother; loved ones stop at nothing,

---

11. It was a common belief that a woman with a large dowry would take
more power in her household than was socially approved (a dowry had to
be returned in the case of divorce).

12. The Acheloüs is the largest river in Greece. Although nowhere near
the scene of the play, it stands for fresh water in general.

they kill each other, since no law prevents them.[13]
Don't bring that kind of practice over here.
It's not right for a man to hold the reins
of two women. If he intends to run   185
his household well, he'll look to just one Cypris[14]
and cherish just one woman in his bed.

CHORUS:
A woman's mind is a thing that's filled with envy
and hate for any rival in her marriage.

ANDROMACHE:
My god.
Youth is a harmful thing for human beings,   190
especially when coupled with injustice.
I'm afraid that since I am your slave
I'll be deterred from speaking, even though
I have a lot to say, and justice prompts me.
Effective words could get me in more trouble: 195
those who bluster really do resent
strong arguments from their inferiors.
Still, I won't betray myself.

                              Young woman,
tell me, what compelling argument
induces me to drive you from your place   200
in a legal marriage? Is Sparta so much weaker
than Phrygia?[15] Am I more fortunate

---

13. Greek mythology is, of course, full of kin-murder and incest (both
are found in Hermione's own family tree). Later Zoroastrianism strongly
endorsed marriage within the nuclear family, but we do not know how
close Persian religion of this period was to later Zoroastrianism. It is,
however, at least possible that Hermione's comments are based on Greek
information about Zoroastrianism or about the practices of the Persian
royal house.

14. Aphrodite is often called Cypris (for Cyprus, where she had an important cult at Paphos; she was supposed to have been born nearby). The name
Aphrodite/Cypris has a variety of metonymic meanings associated with
sex, here "source of sexual satisfaction."

15. Phrygia was an ancient state of west-central Anatolia, in Euripides'
time part of the Persian Empire. Troy was often assimilated to Phrygia.

than you? Look at me. Am I free?[iv] Or is it
that I intend to occupy your house
205 because my youthful body, my great city,
and all the friends and loved ones that surround me
have filled me with so much self-confidence?
Do I want to take your place in bearing children?
They'd be slaves, a burden, a dead weight!
210 Or would the Phthians tolerate my sons
as rulers, if you cannot bear a child?[16]
Oh yes, the Greeks love me for Hector's sake.
Am I unknown? Was I not queen of Phrygia?

It's not my drugs that make your husband hate you;
215 it's just because you're difficult to live with.
Compliance is a kind of magic charm;
it's excellence, not beauty, that delights
our bedmates. You, however, just as soon
as something irritates you, you get started:
220 Laconia is great! Scyros is nothing![17]
You're a patrician trapped here among paupers!
Menelaus, so you claim, is greater
than Achilles ever was. That's why your husband
can't stand you.
                        A woman, even if she's married
225 to someone horrible, must acquiesce,
not fight her man or think defiant thoughts.
Let's say that you'd been married to the king
of Thrace, a land all blanketed in snow,
where one man shares his bed with many women.[18]

---

16. Molossus, the son of Neoptolemus and Andromache, was the legendary ancestor of the kings of the Molossians in Epirus, to the west of the play's setting, which somewhat undercuts Andromache's argument.

17. Laconia is the region whose center is Sparta. Scyros is the birthplace of Neoptolemus. Achilles' mother, who did not want him to die at Troy, hid him among the women on the island of Scyros, where he seduced Neoptolemus' mother.

18. Thrace was the region that is now European Turkey, the northeast corner of Greece, and southeastern Bulgaria. At least some Thracian tribes practiced polygamy; Hermione and Andromache seem to be engaging in competitive ethnography.

Would you have killed the others? If you had,   230
you would have smeared all women with the charge
that we're insatiable in bed.
                              It's a disgrace.
We do have this disease—we're worse than men.
But we know how to put up a good front.
Oh Hector, oh my love. The things I did   235
for your sake!
                    If Cypris had beguiled you,
I went along with it. I gave my breast
to nurse your bastard children, many times;
I never showed a flicker of resentment.

My excellence endeared me to my husband.   240
But you're afraid to let a single droplet
of water from the sky have any contact
with your husband's skin. You shouldn't try
to be more man-crazy than your own mother.
Children of bad mothers ought to shun   245
their wicked ways, if they have any sense.

CHORUS:
Mistress, if you can, I recommend
that you try to go along with what she says.

HERMIONE: (To Andromache.)
Oh, aren't you superior! You say
that you have wise restraint, and I do not?   250

ANDROMACHE:
I say you don't, to judge from your own words.

HERMIONE:
I want no part of what *you* mean by "sense."

ANDROMACHE:
Young girl that you are, you speak of what is shameful.

HERMIONE:
Well, you do more than speak! You're *doing* it.

ANDROMACHE:

255   Will you shut up about your bedroom problems!

HERMIONE:

But—isn't that what counts the most for women?

ANDROMACHE:

Yes,
but nothing's right for women who act wrongly.

HERMIONE:

We don't live by barbarian customs here.

ANDROMACHE:

Both here and there, disgrace is called disgraceful.

HERMIONE:

260   You're very clever. Still, you'll have to die.

ANDROMACHE:

Do you see Thetis' statue watching you?

HERMIONE:

Yes;
she hates your land, because of Achilles' murder.

ANDROMACHE:

Helen—*your* mother!—destroyed him. It wasn't I.

HERMIONE:

Will you keep poking and prodding at my troubles?

ANDROMACHE:

265   No—I'll stop right there. My lips are sealed.

HERMIONE:

Say what I have come to hear you say.

ANDROMACHE:

I say you have no sense. You should think again.[v]

HERMIONE:
Will you leave the sea goddess' sanctuary?

ANDROMACHE:
If I can live. If not, I'll stay forever.

HERMIONE:
This has been settled. I won't wait for my husband.   270

ANDROMACHE:
I won't give in to you before he gets here.

HERMIONE:
I'll bring fire. Your interests don't concern me.

ANDROMACHE:
Bring fire and burn me, then! The gods will see this.

HERMIONE:
I'll wound your body, and you'll feel the pain.

ANDROMACHE:
Go ahead and kill me! Soak this altar   275
with my blood. The goddess will pursue you.

HERMIONE:
Pure, resolute audacity! A true
barbarian born and bred. You're not afraid
of dying? All the same, I'll make you leave
this altar soon enough, of your own will.   280
I have something to lure you. Anyway,
I'll say no more; soon enough the situation
will speak for itself. You could be held in place
with molten lead[19]—still, I will make you leave
before he arrives, the one you're counting on—   285
Achilles' son.

   (Exit Hermione into the house.)

---

19. Greeks used molten lead to attach statues to their bases and as solder
for the clamps that held blocks of masonry fixed together.

ANDROMACHE:
> I'm counting on him, yes.
> It's strange; some god has given to mankind
> a cure for every kind of biting snake,
> but no drug has been found for what is worse
290 than fire, or any viper's venom: woman.[vi]

CHORUS:
[Strophe 1]

> He set into motion unbearable grief, the child of Maia
> and Zeus, when he came to the glade
> on Ida's slopes, driving a beautiful war-team:
> three goddesses, caparisoned in hateful
295 conflict—a beauty contest;[20]
> they came to the young herdsman's hearth,
> lonely, deserted, off in the woods.

[Antistrophe 1]

> They came to the glade on the mountain and bathed their
>   radiant bodies
> with water that flowed from the springs
300 in Ida's forests, and they brought their malignant,
> extravagant proposals; Priam's son was
> tricked by the words of Cypris:
> delightful to hear, but they brought
> bitter annihilation to Troy.

[Strophe 2]

305 If only the mother who bore this evil had flung him away[vii]
> before he came to dwell in Ida's crags,
> when Cassandra cried out for his death
> beside the prophetic laurel,
> denouncing the utter outrage to Priam's city.

---

20. Hermes, son of Zeus and Maia, accompanied the three goddesses whose argument over who was most beautiful led to the Judgment of Paris. Each goddess offered Paris a bribe; Aphrodite's was the most beautiful woman in the world.

Which of the elders did she not approach then,   310
not beg to slaughter the baby?[21]

[Antistrophe 2]

Then slavery's yoke never would have come to descend on the
                                                                  necks
of Trojan women; you, my friend, would live
in a palace; Greece would have been freed
from ten years of toil in Asia—   315
young warriors wandering vainly outside the Trojan
city walls—beds would not have been deserted,
old men not buried their children.

> *(Enter Menelaus with attendants
> and Andromache's child.)*

MENELAUS:
I have your child, whom you placed secretly
in another house, to hide him from my daughter.   320
You felt so sure that you would be kept safe
by this image of the goddess, and your son
by those who hid him. But it seems, my friend,
that Menelaus has more sense than you.
Now, if you don't desert this area,   325
this child will be slaughtered in your place.
Think about it: do you want to die,
or to let him be killed for your wrongdoing,
the wrong you've done to me and to my daughter?

ANDROMACHE:
O Fame! You have inflated the importance   330
of thousands—men who in themselves are worthless.
Those who truly do deserve acclaim,
I call them blessed. But those who have it falsely
I take no heed of; it's nothing more than luck

---

21. In other versions, Paris' mother Hecuba dreamed that she gave birth
to a torch. Paris was exposed but was rescued by a shepherd. Euripides in
415 BCE dramatized how Paris was recognized by his family in the lost
Alexandros, which included a prophecy by Cassandra.

335   that gives them the appearance of good sense.
        A simpleton like you once led the troops,
        the finest men of Greece, and took the city
        of Troy from Priam? Now you're here, all bluster,
        and on the say-so of your childish daughter
340   you're challenging a miserable slave woman
        to a debate. I can no longer see
        how you and Troy ever deserved each other.[viii]
        Menelaus, let's go through this point by point.

        Let's say I've died; your daughter has destroyed me.
345   She won't escape the stain of having murdered.
        And in the people's eyes, you too will be
        charged with murder; you are her accomplice.

        Let's say I live, then. What will you do? Kill
        my child? And will his father just stand by
350   and shrug it off—the murder of his baby?
        Does he seem so unmanned to you? Just ask
        the Trojans; they would disagree. He'll do
        what must be done; he'll prove that he's the son
        of Achilles; he'll be worthy of Peleus.
355   He'll drive your daughter out of his house. And you,
        what will you tell a prospective second husband?
        That she, with all her wisdom and restraint,
        fled an unworthy spouse? He won't believe it.
        Who will marry her? Or will you keep her,
360   gray-haired and unmanned, in your own house?
        You poor man, can't you see that misery
        is opening its floodgates? How many times
        would you rather see your daughter's bed dishonored
        than to endure all that? Don't take small pretexts
365   and turn them into large disasters. If
        a woman is an evil piece of work,
        then men should never imitate our nature.
        And if, as she claims, I am using drugs
        to blast your daughter's womb, then willingly—
370   not clinging to an altar for asylum—
        I'll face whatever charges are brought forward
        by your son-in-law, since he's the injured party
        no less than she, if I have made her childless.
        That's where I stand. There's just one thing I fear

about your way of thinking: you destroyed   375
my Phrygian city because of female conflict.[ix]

CHORUS:
You've said more than a woman ought to say
when speaking to a man. Your wise restraint
abandoned you, shot outward like an arrow.[x]

MENELAUS:
Just as you say, these matters are mere trifles   380
unworthy of my kingship, or of Greece.
But you must realize: what each man needs
at any given time means more to him
than taking Troy. I will stand by my daughter
and be her ally; she has been deprived   385
of her marriage bed, and that means a great deal.
For a woman, no other loss compares:
losing her man means losing her whole life.

That man has the right to rule my slaves;
likewise, my family and I may rule his.   390
No property is private among loved ones;
all things are shared among true friends and family.[22]
I'd be a simpleton, not wise at all,
to wait around for his return. I must
attend to my own interests, set things right.   395
Get up, and leave the goddess' sanctuary.
If you die, then your son escapes his fate.
If you're not willing, he's the one I'll kill.
One or the other of you must leave this life.

ANDROMACHE:
A bitter pair of lots you set before me;   400
either way I lose. I choose between
pure misery and utter devastation.
You're doing great harm, led on by mere trifles.
Listen to me. Why kill me? For whose sake?
What city did I betray? Which of your children   405

---

22. That friends share everything is a Greek commonplace, but Menelaus'
application of the principle is clearly perverse (see 601 below).

did I kill? Whose house did I burn down?
Yes, I slept with my master—I was forced.
So why kill me instead of him, the one
who started all this? Why forget the cause,
410   and focus only on the consequence?
Alas, my sorrows. Oh, my unhappy homeland.
I've suffered terrible things. Why did I have to
bear a child, add burden onto burden?
—But why lament that? I have troubles here,
415   right at my feet, which I must now consider.xi
I, who saw the wheel-drawn death of Hector,
saw Troy in flames, a pitiful sight, and then
was dragged by the hair, a slave, to the Greek ships.
In Phthia, I was married to the family
420   of Hector's murderers. So tell me: how
is my existence sweet? What should I look to?
My past good fortune, or my current joy?
One child is left to me—the precious eye
of my life—and they've decreed that they must kill him.
425   No, not for the sake of my pathetic life!
There's hope for him, if he survives; for me
it would be shameful not to die for him.
Look, I've left the altar. I'm all yours:
slaughter me, slay me, bind me, cut my throat.

430   My child, your mother is on her way to Hades
so you won't die. If you escape your fate
then think of me, your mother—all I've suffered
and how I was destroyed. Embrace your father,
and kiss him—shedding tears, enfolding him
435   in your arms—and tell him everything I've done.

Children are our life, our heart and soul;
that's true for everyone. Some people, who
have no experience, find children tiresome.
They may have less pain, but they are blessed
440   with the fortune of being truly unfortunate.

CHORUS:
I feel pity when I hear these things.
Misfortunes, even an outsider's, move
all human beings to pity. Menelaus,

you ought to reconcile this woman here
with your daughter; you should free her from her toils.   445

MENELAUS:
Servants, take this woman; hold her tight
with your arms around her. She's about to hear
a few unfriendly words.

(Menelaus' slaves seize Andromache.)

                    I have you now.
I held out your son's death to make you leave
the goddess' holy altar; with that threat   450
I drew you to the slaughter, into my hands.
That's how it is for you, you understand.
As for your child, my child will decide
whether or not to kill him. Get inside
that house.
                    Your behavior is an outrage   455
to those who are free. A slave should learn respect.

ANDROMACHE:
You sneak! I've been deceived. You lied to me.

MENELAUS:
I don't deny it. Go ahead, announce it.

ANDROMACHE:
Is this what you call clever back in Sparta?

MENELAUS:
In Troy as well—a sufferer strikes back.   460

ANDROMACHE:
The gods have justice on their side, you know.

MENELAUS:
I'll take whatever comes. I'm going to kill you.

ANDROMACHE:
And the little bird you've torn from under my wing?

MENELAUS:
  I'll give him to my daughter. She'll decide.
  If she wants, she'll kill him.

ANDROMACHE:
465   No—my baby!

MENELAUS:
  It's true, he doesn't stand much of a chance.

ANDROMACHE:
  You Spartans! The whole human race detests you.
  Counselors of deception, masters of lies,
  weavers of evil strategies, contorted
470 and noxious in your twisted deliberations,
  your success in Greece is utterly
  unjustified. What *won't* you stoop to? Don't you
  specialize in murder, shameful gains,
  and saying one thing, with something else in mind?
475 To hell with you.[23] The death you have decreed
  is not so bad for me. The day I died
  was the day my Phrygian city was destroyed
  and my glorious husband, who often with his spear
  drove you from dry land, reduced you to
480 a weakling sailor. Now you're a fearsome warrior
  against a woman! And you're going to kill me.
  Kill me, then! I will not fawn on you
  or on your child. You may be great in Sparta,
  but I was great in Troy. Don't be so smug
485 if I have troubles. You may suffer too.

      *(Exit Menelaus and attendants into the house,
      taking Andromache and the child.)*

CHORUS:
                          [Strophe 1]

  For mortals, I could never recommend
  a twofold bond in the bedroom, or children

---

23. This anti-Spartan tirade (467–75) obviously reflects contemporary
sentiment in Athens and among supporters of Athens' side in the war.

whose mothers compete with each other.
That brings hatred, conflict, and grief to the home.
May my husband find contentment   490
in an unshared marriage bed.

[Antistrophe 1]

Double kingship never works as well
as single rule in a city; it only
creates civil strife, adding burden
onto burden. Conflict is common when two   495
poets try to work together,
and the Muses make them fight.

[Strophe 2]

When swift winds carry sailors along,
a twofold opinion—even a bevy of wise men—
is weaker than a single mind at the rudder,   500
yes, even a simpleton's, if he is in control.
In palaces and cities, one man alone
is best for getting things done at just the right moment.

[Antistrophe 2]

The girl from Sparta demonstrates this—
the general's child, the daughter of King Menelaus—   505
a rival in her bedroom kindles her rage, and
she wants to kill the poor daughter of Troy and her child.
Malignant Conflict!xii Godless, lawless assault!24

My Mistress, one day these deeds will come back to haunt you.

> (Andromache and her child enter from the house with
> Menelaus and attendants. Andromache's hands are
> bound together at the wrists. In the following scene,
> the Chorus and Menelaus chant in anapests, and
> Andromache and her child sing in responsive stanzas.)

---

24. Sparta had two kings, which may help explain this detail in this
somewhat odd song (504–16). The Chorus oppose polygamy because it
inevitably causes strife, then endorse monarchy, even if the single ruler is
not well qualified, because otherwise strife arises. It is not clear how the
political argument fits with the criticism of polygamy.

510   Look! Now I see them, in front of the house,
       the two of them clinging so closely together
       they blend into one. They're condemned by decree;
       they will die.
                        You poor woman! Unfortunate child,
       to die for the sake of a bedroom dispute!
515   It's your mother, not you; in the eyes of our rulers
       you've done nothing wrong.

                        [Strophe]

ANDROMACHE:
    Here I am; they are sending me
    under the earth; they've bound me
    tightly; my arms are bleeding.

CHILD:
520   Mother, Mother! I want to fly
       under your wing for shelter.

ANDROMACHE:
    Lords of Phthia,[25] this sacrifice
    is most violent.

CHILD:
                        Oh Father,
    come now, and save your loved ones!

ANDROMACHE:
525   Oh my child, you will lie with me
       underground, by your mother's breast,
       one corpse next to the other.

CHILD:
    What will happen to me? I'm scared.
    Oh poor me, oh poor mother.

MENELAUS:
530   Go to the Underworld! You're from an enemy
       city, and therefore your death is compulsory,

---

25. The "lords" are the absent Peleus and Neoptolemus.

both of you: *you* die because *I* decreed it;
my daughter Hermione sentenced your child.

It's crazy to leave a survivor, an enemy—
or enemy's child—when you're able to kill them,   535
and thus free your household from terror.

[Antistrophe]

ANDROMACHE:
Oh my husband, I wish I had
you here beside me, Priam's
son, as my ally, fighting!

CHILD:
Poor me! What can I sing? What song   540
could turn aside my fate now?

ANDROMACHE:
Child, you must take your master's knees.
Supplicate him.

(The child throws his arms around Menelaus' knees.)

CHILD:
                    My friend, please!
Don't make me die. Release me.

ANDROMACHE:
Now my eyes overflow with tears   545
like a spring in a sunless place
pouring down a smooth rock face.

CHILD:
Oh my sorrow. How can I find
some way out of these troubles?

MENELAUS:
Why do you fall at my feet? You are wasting your   550
prayers; I am just like a rock, or an ocean wave.
I can be helpful to people I care for;
for you I feel nothing. There's no magic charm

to stir my compassion. I paid with my soul,
555   a piece of my life, taking Troy and your mother.
You'll go down to Hades beside her.

> (Enter Peleus, proceeding slowly with the assistance of
> both a royal scepter, which he uses as a walking stick,
> and an attendant. Here spoken dialogue resumes.)

CHORUS:
Look! I see Peleus. He's coming near;
he's hurrying this way on agèd legs.

PELEUS:
I ask you—all of you, especially
560   the one presiding over this butchery—
What's going on? What is this? What's the reason
for this disease in the household? How can you
employ such thoughtless, knee-jerk strategies?

> (Coming closer and recognizing Menelaus.)

Menelaus! Stop! You are too hasty.
This is unjust.

> (To his attendant.)

565   And you, lead on, now—faster!
This is no time for leisure. I must summon
all the strength I had when I was young,
now more than ever. First of all, I'll fill
this woman's sails, just like a fair wind.
570   Tell me, on what charge are these men binding
your arms with ropes, and leading you away
together with your child? You are destroyed,
a sheep with her young lamb, while we are gone,
your guardian and I.

ANDROMACHE:
                    These men, as you
575   can see, old man, are leading me away
to death, me and my baby. What can I add?

I sent for you, not once but countless times.
Perhaps you've heard about my household conflict
with this man's daughter, and the reasons why
I am destroyed. And now they're leading me   580
away; they've dragged me from the altar of Thetis—
who bore your noble son, whom you revere
and adore—without a formal charge, without
waiting for the ones who aren't at home.
They know we've been deserted, me and my child—   585
who's done nothing wrong!—and they are going to kill him
with me, unhappy woman that I am.

(Andromache falls to her knees in supplication.)

I'm begging you, old man, I'm falling down
before your knees—I cannot use my hand
to touch your beloved beard—please, by the gods,   590
save me. If you don't we'll die, and that
would mean disgrace for you; for me, misfortune.

PELEUS: *(To the attendants.)*
Untie these bonds, or someone will be sorry.
That's an order: release her fettered hands.

MENELAUS:
And I say no. I'm just as powerful   595
as you, and I have more sway over her.

PELEUS:
How's that? Will you come here and rule my household?
You rule in Sparta; isn't that enough?

MENELAUS:
I took her captive; I brought her from Troy.

PELEUS:
She then became my grandson's prize of honor.   600

MENELAUS:
Isn't what's mine his, and what's his mine?

PELEUS:
Yes,
to treat correctly. Not to harm, or kill.

MENELAUS:
You'll never take this woman from my hands.

PELEUS:
Oh no? I'll beat you bloody with this scepter!

MENELAUS:
605   You'll see what happens if you touch me. Try it.

PELEUS:
Are you a man? You are the worst, descended
from trash! How do you figure as a man?
You let your wife go to a Phrygian,
leaving your house unlocked, her bed unguarded,
610   as if she were restrained by her own wisdom—
but she was the worst of all! A Spartan girl
could never, even if she wanted to,
exhibit wise restraint. They bare their thighs,[26]
they go with young men, they desert their homes
615   for wrestling grounds and races, with their clothing
undone. To me, it is unbearable.
So, is it any wonder that you Spartans
can't teach your women wisdom and restraint?
Ask Helen! She left home, abandoned Friendship,[27]
620   and went to party in another land
with her young man. For *her* sake, you assembled
so great a host, and led them off to Troy?
Once you discovered she was trash, you should have
spat her out, not set the spears in motion!
625   You should have let her stay there, should have paid
good money—wages!—to keep her from coming home.

---

26. Young women at Sparta engaged in athletics, wearing clothes that
showed their thighs.
27. Helen abandoned *Philios* ("Friendship"), short for Zeus Philios, the
god of family bonds.

But that's not how the wind blew in your mind.
How many brave men's souls you have destroyed;
you've made old women childless, and taken
noble sons from their old gray-haired fathers.   630
I am one of these, much to my grief.
In my eyes, you're Achilles' murderer.
You are polluted. You're the only one
who came back home unscathed from Troy, your armor
all beautiful and shining, shield wrapped up   635
in its fine case, just like when you left home![28]

I told my grandson not to form a marriage-bond
with you, and not to take into his house
the filly of an evil woman. Mothers
display their faults in future generations.   640
(Young men, take care: be sure to wed the daughter
of a worthy mother!) What's more, you've committed
a terrible outrage against your brother:
at your bidding, like a fool, he killed
his daughter![29] Were you so afraid to lose   645
your miserable wife? Then, when you'd taken
Troy (yes, I will say it:) you had that woman
in your hands, and yet you didn't kill her—
no! When you saw her breast, you dropped your sword
and let her kiss you. How you fawned on her,   650
that bitch, that traitor.[30] You could not withstand
the power of Cypris. Yes, you are the worst.
And then you come here plundering the house
of my own grandchild when he's not at home,
and trying, dishonorably, to kill this poor   655
unfortunate woman and her child. I tell you,
he'll make you sorry one day, you and your daughter;
I don't care if he's three times a bastard!
Often dried-out dirt yields richer harvests

---

28. Homer's Menelaus, though not a leading warrior, is a responsible person and no coward.

29. The army could not sail from Greece because of contrary winds until Agamemnon sacrificed his daughter Iphigenia to Artemis.

30. The story that Menelaus planned to kill Helen but stopped when she bared her breasts was told in the lost epic, the *Little Iliad*.

660   than deep, moist loam, and bastards prove much better
         than legal heirs. Go, take your daughter home.
         A man is better off to have an in-law
         or loved one who is poor and decent, rather
         than rich and despicable. You count for nothing.

CHORUS:
665   The tongue can turn a tiny provocation
         into a huge quarrel. Wise men avoid
         creating any conflict with their loved ones.

MENELAUS:
         How can old men be considered wise?
         Peleus, look at you: descended from
670   a glorious father,[31] you formed a marriage-bond
         with those the Greeks gave credit for good sense;[xiii]
         and yet you say things that reflect on you
         disgracefully; you reproach me for the sake
         of this barbarian woman, whom you should have
675   driven far beyond the Nile's streams,
         beyond the Phasis—and I would have helped you![32]
         She's from the continent, where so many Greeks
         fell to foreign spears; their fallen corpses
         filled that land,[xiv] and she has your son's blood
680   upon her hands, for Paris was the brother
         of Hector, slayer of your son Achilles,
         and she was Hector's wife. And yet you share
         a roof with her, you eat at the same table,
         you let her breed your bitterest enemies![33]
685   And when I had the foresight—looking out

---

31. Peleus' father was the hero Aeacus. His mother was the nymph Aegina.

32. The Phasis was in Colchis, across the Black Sea (now in Georgia). The Phasis and Nile together mark the ends of the earth.

33. Menelaus takes a normal Greek attitude, that it would be repugnant to associate with the killers of a relative or their close relatives, and distorts it. Andromache had nothing to do with Achilles' death. It applies much more to her—she has been forced to cohabit with the son of her husband's killer.

for you as well as for myself, old man—
to want to kill her, she was taken from me.
Now, look—it's no disgrace to point this out—
if my child has no children, and *she* does,
will you set them as rulers over Phthia,   690
barbarians over Greeks? And *I'm* the one
who's empty-headed, just because I hate
what isn't just, and *you're* the one with sense?^{xv}
You are an old, old man. As for the war,
and my command, that point works in my favor.   695

Helen's heartaches didn't arise from her own
free will, but from the gods. And furthermore
this worked in Greece's favor. Hellas was
completely ignorant of arms and warfare;
the army found its way to manliness.   700
Experience is mankind's greatest teacher.
And if I held back when I saw my wife
and didn't kill her, I showed wise restraint.
I wish that you had not killed Phocus, either.³⁴
I come to you in friendship, not in anger.   705
You'll wear your tongue out with your fiery spirit,
while I can only gain by having forethought.

CHORUS:
Hold back these foolish words; they'll be the downfall
of both of you. It's best by far to stop now.

PELEUS:
We have an idiotic custom here   710
in Greece; when armies triumph over foes,
it's not the ones who really did the work
who get the credit: it's the general.
He waved his spear along with countless others,
and did no more than any other man,   715
but he gets more renown. So high and mighty!
They take their seats of office in the city
and think that they are better than the people,

---

34. Peleus was exiled from Aegina after he killed his half-brother Phocus.

but really, they are nobodies.^{xvi} Like you!
720   You and your brother, sitting there, inflated
by Troy and by your generalship there,
so filled with self-importance, thanks to toils
and heartaches borne by others. I'll show you
that Peleus is every bit as much
725   your enemy as Paris ever was
if you don't get the hell away from here
right now. And take your barren daughter with you!
My grandson will get rid of her; he'll drag her
through the house by her hair, if she can't stand
730   for anybody else to have a child
while she has none, since she's a sterile cow.
Why does she have to make *me* childless
because of her own bad luck in that department?
Servants, get the hell away from her!
735   I'd like to see if anyone will stop me
from untying her hands.

          (To Andromache.)

                    Now, raise yourself.
Though I am trembling, I can still untangle
these knotted leather straps.

          *(Andromache rises and Peleus unties
          her as he addresses Menelaus.)*

You are the worst! Just look at how her arms
740   are bruised. What did you think, that you were roping
a steer, or lion? Or were you afraid
she'd take a sword and get back at you?

          (To the child.)

                    Sweetheart,
come here into my arms; help me untie
your mother's bonds. I'll raise you up in Phthia
745   to be these people's mighty enemy.

          (To Menelaus.)

The Spartans' reputation rests on spears

and battles. If you take all that away,
you're just the same as anybody else.

CHORUS:
An old man is a thing that's uncontrolled:
a fiery spirit, not easy to fend off.   750

MENELAUS:
You're too inclined to chastise. I was forced
to come to Phthia; I will not be petty
in my treatment of anyone, nor will I endure
such treatment at another's hands. For now
(since there are limits to my leisure time)   755
I'm going home. There is a certain state
not far from Sparta, previously friendly,
but recently turned hostile. My intention
is to go there with an army and subdue them,
and then, when I have worked things out in that place,   760
I'll come back here. In person, face to face
my son-in-law and I will speak and listen,
teach and be taught. If he will punish *her,*
and if henceforward he shows wise restraint,
he will be treated with wisdom and restraint.   765
If he gets angry, he'll be met with anger;
he will be treated just as he treats us.

The things you say do not affect me much.
You stand there like a shadow with a voice,
unable to do anything but talk.   770

(Exit Menelaus with attendants.)

PELEUS:
Lead on, my child. Stand here beneath my arm
and prop me up. You too, poor woman. After
the wild storm you've been through, you have found
safe harbor here, and shelter from the winds.

ANDROMACHE:
May the gods be kind to you and all your family,   775
most venerable sir. You've saved my child

and poor, unhappy me. Be careful, now:
those men could be in some deserted spot
along the road, lying in wait to take me
780   by force; they see that you are old, I'm weak,
the child is helpless. Be on guard. For now
we have escaped; let's not get caught again.

PELEUS:
That's woman's talk! Don't be a coward. Come on.
Who's going to take you? Anyone who tries
785   will be sorry. I hold power here in Phthia
thanks to the gods, and thanks to cavalry
and infantry, a multitude of men.
Besides, I'm really not so old and weak.
I can triumph over a man like that
790   with just one glance—senior that I am!
An old man, if he's fearless, can defeat
a pack of younger men. What good is strength
and vigor, if you're nothing but a coward?

(Exit Peleus with attendant, Andromache, and the child.)

CHORUS:
[Strophe]

Let me be born to noble and wealthy parents
795   and a home piled high with riches,
or never be born at all.
Aristocrats are shielded from suffering
where others have no recourse.
Good families, whose names are read in proclamations,
800   have honor and glory. Time cannot erase them.
Their excellence shines out, even after death.

[Antistrophe]

Honest defeat is better than victory tainted
with injustice, violence, grudges.
At first this is sweet; in time
805   it dries out and tastes stale, and the household's stuck
with scandals and reproaches.
The life that I praise, the life that I aspire to

is one that does not wield power divorced from justice
in private rooms at home, or in public life.

[Epode]

Old man, Aeacus' son,   810
I can believe that you fought with your glorious spear
by the Lapiths' side, against the Centaurs,
and that you plied the inhospitable waters
and sailed through the Clashing Rocks of Pontus
aboard the Argo, on that glorious voyage,   815
and that, when Zeus's son
long ago wrapped the glorious city of Troy
in slaughter, you came home
to Europe with your share of the acclaim.[35]

(Enter Hermione's Nurse from the house.)

NURSE:
Dearest women, this day brings us trouble   820
on top of trouble. Hermione, my mistress,
wants to die; deserted by her father,
regretful over what she's done—her plot
to kill Andromache and her young child—
she fears her husband; she's afraid he might   825
expel her with dishonor from this house
or kill her, since she wrongly tried to kill.
The servants watching her can barely keep her
from trying to hang herself; they've had to grab
the sword out of her hand and take it from her,   830
so great is her remorse and her awareness
that what she did was wrong. My friends, I'm tired:
worn out from keeping the noose off of her neck![36]
Go inside yourselves, and see if you
can save her from her death. She's used to me;   835
somebody new would be much more persuasive!

---

35. Peleus' heroic achievements (810–19): he fought with the Lapiths
against the Centaurs; he was an Argonaut; and he participated in the first
Trojan War, when Heracles sacked the city.

36. Hanging is the typical form of women's suicide in Greek tragedy.

CHORUS:
I do hear servants shouting in the house
about the things you said. Unhappy woman!
She'll let us see just how much she bemoans
840   her terrible deeds. She's coming outside now,
fleeing the servants in her desire for death.

(*Enter Hermione from the house. In the following
passage Hermione sings and the Nurse speaks.*)

HERMIONE:

[Strophe 1]

Poor me, oh poor me!
I will tear out my tresses,
I'll gouge myself with violent nails!

NURSE:
845   My child, what are you doing? Don't deface yourself!

HERMIONE:

[Antistrophe 1]

Alas, oh alas!
Go, my fine-woven kerchief,
fly off my hair, into the air!

NURSE:
Child, cover up your bosom! Fix your garments.

HERMIONE:

[Strophe 2]

850   Why should I hide my bosom?
What I have done to my husband
is revealed, and uncovered, and clear!

NURSE:
Your murder plot against his other wife . . . ?

HERMIONE:

[Antistrophe 2]

Yes, I regret my violent
daring, my deeds, my accursèd   855
and detestable, damnable self!

NURSE:

You've done wrong, but your husband will forgive you.

HERMIONE:

Why do you grab the sword
out of my hand? Get back!
Get back, my friend, and let me drive home this deathblow.   860
Why keep me away from the noose?

NURSE:

I can't just let you die. Your mind's not right.

HERMIONE:

Alas for my fate!
May a firebolt strike me now!
May I leap from a lofty rock   865
into the sea, or a forested mountain crag,
and unite with the dead below.

NURSE:

Why all this heartache? Every human being
receives his share of disasters from the gods.

HERMIONE:

You left me, you left me, Father,   870
alone on the shore, deserted,
a boat with no oar.
My husband will surely kill me.
I'll no longer live in my bridal
home. Where shall I take refuge,   875
what god's sacred image?
Shall I be a slave, and fall at the knees of a slave?

I wish I could be
a dark-winged bird, flying away from Phthia,
880   there where the pinewood hull
slipped through the high dark cliffs
on the very first sea voyage.[37]

NURSE:
My child, I didn't approve of your excesses
earlier, when you wronged the Trojan woman,
885   nor do I think you're being reasonable
right now; your fear is exaggerated. Why
would your husband break his marriage-bond with you
over a barbarian woman's worthless words?
You're no captive that he took from Troy:
890   you're the daughter of a noble man; you came here
with loads of gifts; you're from a city blessed
with more than average fortune, and your father,
despite your fears, won't let you down. He won't
allow you to be banished from your home.
895   For now, go back inside! Don't stand out here
for anyone to see, outside the house.
It's shameful to be seen outdoors like this.[38]

(Exit the Nurse back into the house.)

CHORUS:
Look, someone's coming now, in quite a rush:
a foreigner, to judge by his complexion.[39]

(Enter Orestes.)

---

37. The first ship was the *Argo,* which sailed from Iolcus (about 65 kilo-
meters or 39 miles to the east of Phthia).

38. Women were supposed to stay indoors as much as possible. Since
tragedies always take place outside, the plays ignore possible impropriety
unless it is thematically relevant, as it is here. Since Hermione is distraught
and her clothing is disheveled, it is especially inappropriate for her to be
outdoors.

39. It is unclear why Orestes looks obviously foreign, when his uncle
Menelaus apparently did not.

ORESTES:
Women of this land, is this the home   900
and royal palace of Achilles' son?

CHORUS:
You recognize it rightly. Who are you?

ORESTES:
The child of Agamemnon and Clytemnestra.
Orestes is my name. I'm on my way
to Dodona and the oracle of Zeus.[40]   905
When I arrived in Phthia, I decided
to see about my relative: is she living,
does she enjoy good fortune? She's from Sparta—
Hermione. Although she's far away
from where we live, she's very dear to us.   910

HERMIONE:

*(Rushing toward Orestes and putting
her arms around his knees.)*

You're like a harbor in a storm to sailors!
O child of Agamemnon, by your knees:
take pity on me! As you see, my fortunes
are low right now. My arms, like sacred garlands,
enfold your knees; I am your suppliant.[41]   915

ORESTES:
Ah!
What's this? Am I mistaken? Could this be
the mistress of the house, Menelaus' daughter?

---

40. Dodona, the rival of Delphi as the most important oracle in Greece, is in Epirus, in northwest Greece. Although Phthia is plausibly on the way there, Orestes is surely lying, since he has no hesitation in offering to take Hermione home to Sparta.

41. Wreaths or ribbons wound around a branch were suppliants' equipment.

HERMIONE:
  The very one the child of Tyndareos,
  Helen, bore to my father. You can be sure.

ORESTES:
920   O Phoebus, god of healing, grant release!
  What's this? Do gods or mortals make you suffer?

HERMIONE:
  Some troubles are my own doing, some my husband's,
  and some the work of a god. I'm utterly ruined.

ORESTES:
  What else—if you have not borne children yet—
925   could this disaster be than bedroom woes?

HERMIONE:
  You've touched on my distress with great precision.

ORESTES:
  Your husband cherishes another bed?

HERMIONE:
  Yes; the captive woman, Hector's bedmate.

ORESTES:
  That's not a good thing—one man in two beds.

HERMIONE:
930   Exactly. I took steps in self-defense.

ORESTES:
  You wove a womanish plot against the woman?

HERMIONE:
  I planned to kill her, and her bastard child.

ORESTES:
  And did you slay them, or did something stop you?

HERMIONE:
The old man, Peleus—honoring the weaker.

ORESTES:
Did anyone conspire with you to kill them?   935

HERMIONE:
My father came from Sparta just for that.

ORESTES:
And then he failed? The old man strong-armed him?

HERMIONE:
His reverence stopped him. He deserted me.

ORESTES:
I understand. You fear your husband now.

HERMIONE:
You recognize this rightly. He'll destroy me   940
with justice on his side. What can I say?
But I beseech you, by Zeus the god of kinship,
please, send me far away, far from this land,
or back to my paternal home. This house
seems to have a voice that drives me off;   945
the land of Phthia hates me. If my husband
returns from Phoebus' oracle before
I leave here, he will kill me in disgrace,
or else I'll be enslaved to my former slave,
subject to his illegitimate mate.   950

ORESTES:
What led you to do wrong—as some might say?xvii

HERMIONE:
I was destroyed by visits from evil women
who whipped me into a lather with their words:
"How can you stand to share your home and bed
with her, a captive, the lowest of the low?   955
By Hera, if she tried to poach on *my* bed
she'd never see the light of day again."

I listened to their talk, their Siren song—[42]
their embroidered words! their clever, wicked chatter!—[xviii]
960   idiot that I was. They filled my head
with air. Why did I need to guard my husband?
I had all I needed; we had wealth,
and plenty of it; as mistress of the house
my children would have been legitimate
965   while hers, as bastards, would have practically
been slaves to mine.
                               A man with any sense
who has a wife should never, never ever
(I'll say this more than once) let women in
to spend time with his wife at home. They teach
970   all kinds of evil. One woman will corrupt
another's marriage bed for the sake of gain;
another woman has done wrong herself
and wants someone to share in her affliction—
and many act from sheer depravity.
975   This is the source of men's distress at home.
Guard well, therefore, with bolts and bars, the doors
of your houses: visits from outside, from women,
are noxious—they bring evil in abundance.

CHORUS:
You've hurled your words too freely at your own kind.
980   It's understandable, but still, a woman
should put a better face on women's afflictions.

ORESTES:
Somebody once gave this wise advice:
listen to what the other side is saying.
I knew of the confusion in this household,
985   and of your conflict with the wife of Hector;
I watched and waited, wondering if you
would stay here, or would want to leave this house,
in fear because of everything that happened
with the captive woman. It was not to honor
990   any request or message you had sent

---

42. The Sirens' song lured sailors to shipwreck and death.

that I came here, but hoping to have a word
with you, which you have granted, and intending
to take you from this house. For you were mine
before. You live with this man now because
of malfeasance on your father's part; before   995
invading Troy, he promised me your hand
in marriage, but he promised you again
to the one who has you now, as a reward
for ravaging the city.[43] When the son
of Achilles came back home, here to this land,   1000
I understood your father's point of view,
but I begged the other[xix] to give you up, release
his marriage claims. I told him of my fortunes,
the fate that had descended on me, how
I might be able to marry within our circle   1005
of loved ones, but it would be difficult
outside of that, because I was an exile,
because of the house I'd fled from.[44] He, in turn,
insulted me, reproached me, outraged me:
he threw my mother's murder in my face   1010
and the blood-eyed goddesses.[45] I was humiliated
by what had happened in my house. I grieved,
I grieved, but I put up with this disaster,
and left, against my will, without my bride.
Now, I see, your fortunes have collapsed;   1015

---

43. It was standard tradition that Hermione married Orestes after Neoptolemus' death, but the details of her two marriages varied. In tragedies of Philocles (Aeschylus' nephew) and Theognis (a tragedian of the second half of the fifth century BCE, not the famous elegaic poet), she was already pregnant by Orestes when she was married to Neoptolemus. In Sophocles' *Hermione,* her grandfather Tyndareos gave her to Orestes while her father was at Troy, and Menelaus married her to Neoptolemus when he came home. Euripides may have been the first to make Menelaus himself break his own promise.

44. Orestes, in vengeance for his mother's killing of his father, murdered his mother. Hence, he argues, outsiders would not want to ally themselves with him in marriage. Although the play is generally sympathetic to Neoptolemus, he does not seem to have been thoughtful or generous.

45. The "blood-eyed goddesses" are the Furies, who pursued Orestes for killing his mother.

you're facing a disaster with no recourse.
I'll take you home, return you to your father.
Kinship is a terribly potent thing.
When you have troubles, there is nothing stronger
1020   than someone from the family: a loved one.

HERMIONE:
As far as marriage goes, it's not for me
to judge; my father will take care of that.
For right now, hurry! Take me from this house
as quickly as you can, before my husband
1025   gets here and grabs me, or the old man learns
that I've deserted the house, and comes this way
to track us down with chariot and horses.

ORESTES:
Don't fear an old man's strength. As for the son
of Achilles—what an outrage he's committed
1030   against me!—don't fear him at all. I've woven
with my own hand a strategy, a noose
that he cannot escape; his death is fixed.
I will not speak of it beforehand, but
when this is done, the Delphic rock will know.
1035   *If* my spear-companions keep their oath
in Pytho, then this "mother-killer" here
will teach him not to steal a bride that's mine.
He'll bitterly regret that he demanded
amends from Phoebus for his father's death.
1040   His change of heart, the fact that he's now making
amends himself, won't help him. He will die
disgracefully, thanks to my words against him
and thanks to Lord Apollo. He'll find out
what it means to be my enemy.
1045   The gods don't give their enemies a chance
at arrogance. They overturn their fates.

(*Exit Orestes and Hermione in the direction of the
road south. While the Chorus sing, Peleus enters with
his retinue, including Andromache and the child.*)

CHORUS:

[Strophe 1]

Phoebus, who built the towers
transforming Ilion's rocky heights
to a beautiful walled citadel;
Sea lord, I ask you too, who drive   1050
dark horses over the brine,
how could you care so little
for the work of your own hands,
deliver it up to the war god's spear,
and abandon poor, poor Troy?[46]   1055

[Antistrophe 1]

Thousands of chariots
beside the banks of the Simoïs
were equipped and yoked to beautiful
horses; the two of you ordained
a thousand murderous games   1060
whose winners received no garlands.
Now the kings of Troy are dead
and gone, now the altars no longer blaze
for the gods with fragrant smoke.

[Strophe 2]

Gone, too, is the son of Atreus[47]   1065
by the handiwork of his own wife! And she
made her own exchange: with his slaughter, she bought
death at her children's hands.
The god, the god, turned his oracle's bidding against her
when Agamemnon's whelp   1070

---

46. Poseidon, the "sea lord" of 1050, says at *Iliad* 21.441–57 that he built
the walls of Troy while Apollo herded cattle for King Laomedon. The
king, however, refused to pay them and insulted them (Poseidon does not
understand, therefore, why Apollo helps the Trojans). At *Iliad* 7.452–53,
however, Poseidon says that he and Apollo both built the walls. Evidently
there were different versions.

47. Agamemnon. Although Atreus had two sons, Agamemnon and
Menelaus, "son of Atreus" is always Agamemnon.

went straight from the holy sanctuary to Argos
to become his mother's killer.xx
O divine Phoebus, how can I believe this?

[Antistrophe 2]

Groans echoed through every market square
1075   as the unhappy children of Greece sang songs
of bereavement. Wives left their homes and moved on
to somebody else's bed.
It wasn't you and your family alone who were stricken;
malignant pain prevailed.
1080   A plague is what Greece endured: a plague, an affliction.
And it struck the land of Phrygia:
beautiful, fruitful fields were sparged with slaughter.

PELEUS:
Women of Phthia, I ask for information.
I heard a message that was not quite clear,
1085   that Menelaus' daughter has left this house
and gone away. I'm eager to find out
if this is true. The family must take care
to act on behalf of those who aren't at home.

CHORUS:
Peleus, you heard clearly. It's not right
1090   for me to hide the troubles going on here.
The queen has fled, departed from this house.

PELEUS:
What is she afraid of? Tell me that.

CHORUS:
She fears her husband will drive her from the house.

PELEUS:
Because of her deadly plot against the child?

CHORUS:
1095   Yes, and her plan to kill the captive woman.

PELEUS:
Did she leave home with her father? Or someone else?

CHORUS:
Agamemnon's son escorted her from this land.

PELEUS:
What is he hoping for? To marry her?

CHORUS:
Yes, and to carry out your grandson's death.

PELEUS:
In hidden ambush, or face to face in battle?   1100

CHORUS:
In Loxias' holy shrine, with the Delphians.

PELEUS:
Oh no. This is terrible. Can't somebody go
right now, and travel to the Pythian hearth
and tell our loved ones there what's going on
before our enemies kill Achilles' son?   1105

(Enter a Messenger.)

MESSENGER:
Oh god; oh no.
It grieves me, the misfortune I must tell
to you, old man, and to my master's loved ones.

PELEUS:
Aah.
My spirit can foresee what's coming next.

MESSENGER:
Old Peleus, you have to know: your grandson
exists no more. He felt the dagger blows   1110
of Delphians, and the Mycenaean traveler.

(Peleus becomes unsteady on his feet and begins to fall.)

CHORUS:
  Oh no, what's happening? Don't fall, old man!
  Raise yourself!

PELEUS:
                    I count for nothing now.
  I am destroyed. Where is my voice? Where are
  my limbs beneath me?

MESSENGER:
1115   If you really want
  to help your loved ones, get up and hear what happened.

PELEUS:
  O fate, you have enfolded me and hold
  me here, unhappy, in my extreme old age.
  How did my only child's only child
1120 depart from life? I cannot bear to listen
  to what you'll say, and yet I want to hear.

MESSENGER:
  When we arrived at Phoebus' glorious precinct
  we filled three shining orbits of the sun
  with sightseeing, and taking it all in.
1125 Apparently, this made us look suspicious.
  The locals—the god's land's inhabitants—
  began to gather into little groups.
  Agamemnon's son went through the town
  and whispered hateful words in every ear:
1130 "You see this man here, going through the god's
  enclosures crammed with gold, the treasuries
  of mortal men? He's here with the intention
  of sacking Phoebus' temple, just like last time."
  An agitated flurry gathered force
1135 from these beginnings: magistrates rushed in
  to council chambers; citizens in charge
  of the god's coffers took it upon themselves
  to post guards at the columned storehouses.[48]

---

48. In one version of the story, Neoptolemus came to Delphi (once; only
in Euripides does he visit twice) to rob the (immensely wealthy) shrine.

But all of this was still unknown to us.
We got some sheep, raised on the greenery   1140
of Mount Parnassus, and brought them to the altar;
there we stood, with the Pythian guides and prophets.
"Young man," said one of them, "what shall we ask
the god on your behalf? Why have you come?"
He said, "I want to offer my amends   1145
to Phoebus for the wrong I did to him
before, when I asked *him* to make amends
to *me* for my father's blood."
      And that is when
we realized the power of the lies
Orestes had been spreading about my master,   1150
the story that he'd come there to do harm.

He climbed the temple steps and went inside
the inner shrine, so he could pray to Phoebus.
He was making his burnt offering, and then
out of the blue, men with swords! Concealed   1155
by laurel branches, they had lain in wait.
The son of Clytemnestra was among them,
the one who'd woven this whole strategy.[xxi]
Achilles' son was praying to the god
in plain view. They snuck up on him with sharpened   1160
daggers; he was unarmed. They stabbed at him
and he pulled back; their blows had not struck home.
He staggered to the wall, and grabbed the armor[49]
that hung there from a peg. He took his stand—
a fearsome warrior!—upon the altar,   1165
and shouted out these words to the sons of Delphi:

"My journey here is pious! On what charge
are you trying to kill me? You must have a reason
for wanting to destroy me!"

The Messenger's speech includes this detail, even though Neoptolemus
in this version offended Apollo by demanding compensation for Achilles'
death. The atmosphere is typical of the Peloponnesian War: civic panic,
wild rumors, and violence.

49. Armor was often dedicated in temples, so it is not surprising that he
is able to find it.

                                   No one spoke
1170   a word, although a vast crowd swarmed around him;
        they pelted him with rocks. From every side
        they pounded him; he stood there in the midst
        of their barrage—stones flying like a blizzard!—
        warding off the blows, his arms in motion,
1175   parrying with his shield—for all the good
        it did him.[xxii] Still, he managed to deflect
        a shower of weapons: arrows, javelins,
        sharp spits pulled from consecrated victims—
        all fell at his feet. Your boy kept up
1180   his Pyrrhic dance with fierce determination,[50]
        dodging every missile. When the circle
        around him tightened, and he couldn't breathe,
        he left the sacrificial altar,[xxiii] thrusting
        with both his feet—the famous Trojan Leap!—[51]
1185   and sprang toward them. They scattered, just as doves
        will flee in terror when they've seen a hawk.
        Then many of them fell: some of them wounded
        and others trampled in the narrow doorways.
        The shrine, where holy silence should have reigned,
1190   was filled with an unholy din that echoed
        back from the rocks. Then, somehow, it was calm;
        my master stood there in his shining armor.

        A terrible voice rang from the inner sanctum—
        enough to freeze your nerves.[52] It roused the crowd
1195   and turned them back to battle, and the son
        of Achilles fell, taking a blow to the ribs
        from a sharpened dagger held by a Delphian man
        who killed him with the help of many others.[xxiv]
        His body fell to the ground. Then, who among them

---

50. The name of the warlike pyrrhic dance was sometimes derived from
Neoptolemus' other name, Pyrrhus ("red").

51. The Trojan Leap was evidently a familiar fighting maneuver, but we
do not know the story behind it. It must have involved either Achilles or
Neoptolemus.

52. Apollo himself intervenes to ensure Neoptolemus' death. The narrative
is designed to make Neoptolemus as heroic as possible, and to highlight
Apollo's vindictiveness.

did not grab iron and stones, battering him,   1200
bashing him? His body was demolished,
his lovely form defaced with savage wounds.
His corpse lay near the altar; they cast it out
from the temple with its incense-heavy air.

We didn't waste time; we took him in our arms   1205
and bring him to you now, old man, to mourn,
to weep for, and to honor with a grave.

The lord of prophecy, who judges mortals
according to the justice of their actions,
did this to Achilles' son, who was making amends.   1210
The god held onto grudges, like a mean
and petty man. How, then, can he be wise?

(Enter attendants carrying the body of Neoptolemus.)

CHORUS:
Here's our lord coming back
from the Delphian land,
carried homeward by others.   1215

Poor unfortunate sufferer!
Poor *you,* old man!
This is not how you wanted
to welcome him home,
the cub of Achilles.   1220
You have met with a fate
just as dismal as his.

PELEUS:

[Strophe 1]xxv

Oh, this is terrible. What a catastrophe
I see, and touch with my own hand
in my own home. O Thessaly,   1225
it's over now; we are destroyed.
My family is gone: no children are left at home now.
I've suffered so much; there's nowhere my gaze can turn
to find a loved one, a person who delights me.
O beloved mouth, and cheek, and hands,   1230

if only your fortune[53] had struck you down
by Simoïs' riverbanks, back in Troy!

CHORUS:
Old man, he would have honor in his death
that way, and you would be more fortunate.

PELEUS:
[Antistrophe 1]

1235   Marriage, O marriage, you've ruined my household and
destroyed my city, destroyed it.
If only you had never wrapped
my family up in that bad match
for children and home—but not worth the ignominy!
1240   Hermione sent you down to the Underworld,
my child; if only a lightning bolt had killed her!
You were mortal; you should not have charged
Apollo, a god, with the lethal shot
that slew your father, descended from Zeus.[54]

CHORUS:
[Strophe 2]

1245   Woe, and heartbreak! I'll honor my master
with the groans that we owe the dead.

PELEUS:
Woe, and heartbreak! And I, in my grief, will
shed a torrent of old man's tears.

CHORUS:
A god decreed this fate, brought this disaster.

---

53. "Fortune" here (1182 Greek) translates the Greek word *daimon*, which
can mean a god, an attendant spirit, or a person's individual fortune or
destiny. Andromache uses the same word of her fortune at 105 (98 Greek),
and Orestes of his fate in 1004 (974 Greek; cf. Euripides, *Alcestis* 561
[597 AS]).
54. Zeus was the father of Aeacus, Peleus' father.

PELEUS:
Beloved grandson, you left the house deserted;   1250
alas, unhappy me—
you left behind a childless old man.

CHORUS:
You are an elder! You should have died before,
died before your children.

PELEUS:
Let me tear my hair out!   1255
Let me strike my own head now
with a violent hand! O my city,
Apollo has taken two children from me.

CHORUS:

[Antistrophe 2]

All you've seen, all you've suffered is dreadful.
What is left to your days, old man?   1260

PELEUS:
There's no end to my pain. I'm deserted;
I will grieve till I die, bereft.

CHORUS:
The gods who blessed your wedding spoke in vain.

PELEUS:
All that is gone, flown away, beyond the reach of

. . . .

those lofty words, so brimming with pride.[xxvi]   1265

CHORUS:
You're all alone now. You'll end your days alone
in an empty dwelling.

PELEUS:
I have no more city.
What's the use of this scepter?

(Peleus throws his scepter to the ground.)

1270   You can see I'm utterly broken,
        O daughter of Nereus in your dark cave!⁵⁵

(Thetis approaches, flying through the air.)

CHORUS:
        What's that I see moving?
        What's that sound? What divinity
        hastens this way? O women, look there!
1275   Some god is approaching
        the pastures of Phthia
        borne aloft through the luminous air!

(Thetis alights on the roof and addresses Peleus.)

THETIS:
        Peleus, it's me: your goddess, Thetis.
        I've left the halls of Nereus and come here
1280   remembering our former wedded union.
        My first advice to you is: don't resent
        the troubles that beset you. Look at me:
        my father is a god and I'm a goddess;^{xxvii}
        I never should have had to shed a tear
1285   for any child I bore, but I lost yours:
        swift-footed Achilles, greatest of the Greeks.

        I'll tell you why I came here. You must listen.
        Bury Achilles' son at the Pythian altar
        as a reproach to all the Delphians.
1290   His grave will tell the story of his murder,
        the violent death he met at Orestes' hands.

        As for the captive woman Andromache,

---

55. The cave beneath the sea where Thetis lives with her father, though it could also suggest the version of the marriage of Peleus and Thetis in which he had to capture her in a cave and hold her through repeated metamorphoses. Peleus stresses Thetis' distance from him just before she appears, and from the sky (she could not come from the sea in any case, since the setting is inland). The Athenian theater used a crane for such flying appearances, the *mêchanê* (hence the expression "god from the machine").

she must change her home and bed companion:
marry Helenus,[56] settle in Molossia
and live there with this child, the last one left   1295
of Aeacus' descendants.[57] He must be
the founder of a line of kings to rule
Molossia, blessed with fortune. Your family
and mine, old man, must not be blotted out—
and Troy must live. The gods still care for Troy,   1300
although it fell by Pallas Athena's plans.

And you, who shared my bed, will be rewarded:
I'll free you from your human suffering
and make you an immortal, unperishing god.[58]
You'll live with me from this day forth, together,   1305
god with goddess, in the halls of Nereus.
From there you'll step—like walking on dry land!—
across the waves, and see our cherished son
Achilles, dwelling on the coast of Leukê,
a luminous isle of the inhospitable sea.[59]   1310

Now, go to Delphi, the city built by gods.
Carry this body there, cover it with earth,
then make your way to Sepias' jagged coast[60]

---

56. Helenus was a son of Priam who had prophetic abilities. Captured by
the Greeks, he told them what they needed to do in order finally to take
Troy.

57. It should not be strictly true that this son (elsewhere named Molossus)
is the only descendant of Aeacus, since the sons of Peleus' brother Telamon,
Ajax and Teucer, were claimed as ancestors by the Philaid clan in Athens
and by kings on Cyprus, respectively. But the exaggeration is to be taken
as true within the world of the play.

58. Euripides probably invented the immortalization of Peleus, who was
not worshiped as a god.

59. While Peleus' immortality is an invention, already in the post-Homeric
epic *Aethiopis* Achilles after his death was transported to Leukê, the White
Island. This was identified with an island in the Black Sea near the mouth
of the Danube (now in Ukraine, known as Snake Island); Achilles was
widely worshiped in the Black Sea region.

60. Cape Sepias, where in local tradition Peleus "snatched" Thetis
(Herodotus 7.191), is on the eastern shore of the peninsula that forms the
eastern side of the Bay of Volos and is occupied by Mount Pelion.

and sit there in a hollow cave among
1315   the ancient rocks, until I come for you
bringing fifty Nereids from the sea,
a chorus to carry you! For Zeus ordained this,
and you must carry out what has been fated.

Stop grieving for the dead. The gods decreed
1320   that all must die; that goes for everyone.[61]

> *(Thetis begins to fly away in the*
> *direction from which she came.)*

PELEUS:
My Mistress, Holy One, my noble consort,
child of Nereus, farewell. These things you do
are worthy of yourself and your descendants.
As you command, I will no longer grieve;
1325   I'll bury this man, as you ask, and then
I'll go to the folds beneath Mount Pelion
where first my arms embraced your lovely body.

Beyond a doubt, a man who plans things well
must marry nobly, and give his children's hands
1330   to honorable families, never craving
a wrongful match for the sake of golden gifts.[xxviii]

> *(Exit Peleus, Andromache and the child, the Messenger,*
> *and attendants with the body of Neoptolemus.)*

CHORUS:
The designs of the deities take many forms;
they often accomplish what no one would hope for.
What we expect may not happen at all,
1335   while the gods find a way, against all expectation,
to do what they want, however surprising.
And that is exactly how this case turned out.[xxix]

---

61. Although the universality of death is a Greek cliché, it sounds very odd
here, following the announcement of Peleus' immortalization.

Hecuba

Hecuba: Cast of Characters

GHOST OF POLYDORUS	son of Hecuba
HECUBA	queen of Troy
CHORUS	women of Troy, now captives of the Greek army
POLYXENA	daughter of Hecuba
ODYSSEUS	of Ithaca, Greek general
TALTHYBIUS	Greek herald
SERVANT	of Hecuba, an elderly woman
AGAMEMNON	commander of the Greek expedition
POLYMESTOR	king of Thrace

Hecuba

SCENE: *In the Greek army's camp on the Thracian*
           Chersonese, the peninsula across the Hellespont
           from Troy.[1] *One side entrance leads to the*
           main part of the Greek camp; the other leads
           to the seashore. The stage building represents
           Agamemnon's tent, inside which Hecuba is sleep-
           ing; Polydorus' ghost stands in front of the tent.[i]

GHOST OF POLYDORUS:
   I've left the dark recesses of the dead—
   where Hades dwells apart from other gods—
   and crossed the gate of shadows, to come here.
   I'm Polydorus, son of Cisseus' daughter
   Hecuba. My father Priam sent me   5
   out of danger when our city, held
   at spearpoint by the Greeks, came close to falling.
   Priam feared for me, and so I left
   the land of Troy to live with Polymestor,
   my Thracian host, whose spear protects the fruitful   10
   plain of the Chersonese and all its people,
   lovers of horses. My father sent, in secret,
   a large amount of gold with me: he hoped
   that if the walls of Troy should fall, his children,
   if they survived, would be provided for.   15
   I was Priam's youngest, and that's why
   he sent me out of danger. My frame was too slight
   for defensive gear, my arm too young for a sword.

   As long as Troy stayed safe, her towers standing,
   as long as my brother Hector's spear held sway,   20
   my Thracian host—my father's friend—took care
   to raise me well; I flourished like a sapling,
   for nothing.

---

1. The play never explains why the Greek army has sailed across the
Hellespont.

            Then, when Hector was destroyed
      along with Troy—my father's hearth demolished,
25   my father fallen at the god-built altar,
      slaughtered by Achilles' murderous child—[2]
      he killed me for the sake of gold—my host,
      my father's friend!—unhappy me. He threw
      my corpse into the salt waves of the sea
30   so he could keep the gold in his own house.

      One moment I am lying on the shore;
      the next, the surf has rolled me out of reach:
      out and back, like a sprinter running a course
      over and over, unburied and unwept.

35   But now I've deserted my body; I dart above
      the head of my mother Hecuba, suspended
      in space for three days, ever since she left
      her home in Troy, poor thing, and came to this land,
      the Chersonese. The Greeks all sit at rest
40   beside their ships along the Thracian shore,
      heeding an apparition: Peleus' son
      Achilles rose up from his tomb and stopped
      the whole Greek army as they put to sea.
      He demands a blood-offering for his tomb,
45   my sister as his special prize of honor:
      Polyxena.[3] He'll get her. Achilles' friends
      won't let him go without his gift. And fate
      will lead my sister to her death before
      this day is done. My mother's eyes will see
50   two dead bodies, her two children: me
      and that poor girl. I will appear! I want
      a burial, after all that I've been through.
      I'll wash up in the waves between the feet
      of a servant woman. I begged the gods below
55   to let me have a tomb, to let me fall

---

2. The killing of the old king Priam at the household altar by Neoptolemus
(also called Pyrrhus), the son of Achilles, was a well-known atrocity.

3. Achilles had seen Polyxena when he ambushed her and her brother
Troilus; he pursued Troilus and killed him. The story of her sacrifice was
told in the (now lost) epic *Sack of Troy*.

into my mother's arms, and I will have
my wish. But now, I'll get out of the way:
my agèd mother Hecuba emerges
from Agamemnon's tent. My ghost has spooked her.
Ah.
O Mother, from a royal household—you   60
who look upon your day of slavery—
some god has counterpoised your former joy
with all the weight of what you suffer now.

> *(Enter Hecuba from the tent, supported by her*
> *Servant and an attendant. Exit Ghost of Polydorus.)*

HECUBA:
Hold me steady there, children, and help me go out.
Keep me straight! That's the way. I'm not young anymore,   65
dear daughters of Troy; I'm a servant like you,
though I once was your mistress.[ii]

Take ahold of this old lady's arm, and I'll hurry
just as much as I can, in my slow-footed way,
with the crook of your arm as my crutch.   70

> *(Hecuba sings.)*[iii]

Blazing sunlight of Zeus, and obsidian Night,
when will phantoms and night terrors leave me alone?
O Holy One, Earth below, mother of black-wingèd
dreams, may the vision I saw in the night
stay away, leave me be![4]   75

There, in my dream, was my child, whom I sent off to Thrace
                                        for safekeeping;
there was Polyxena, too—my dear daughter appeared in this
                                        vision—
and it shook me with panic.[iv]

Gods of earth down below, keep my child safe from harm!
He alone is my anchor. A friend of his father   80
watches over him now, here in Thrace, land of snow.

---

4. It was a Greek popular belief that the best way to dispel evil omens from
bad dreams was to tell them to the sun and the gods.

How I fear what comes next.

Our refrain will be wailing. We're wailing already.
I'm quailing and trembling like never before.
85   The gods granted Helenus insight—where is he?[5]
Where's my Cassandra?[6] O daughters of Troy,
where's the judge who can help me decipher these dreams?

Here's what I saw in my vision: a dappled deer being
                                    slaughtered,
slain by a wolf's bloody claw, and then torn from my knees
                                    without pity.[v]

90   This is what I am dreading:

from the height of his tomb came the ghost of Achilles
demanding a prize in his honor: a daughter
of Troy, one of those who have known so much heartache.
I beg you, O gods, keep this threat far away
95   from my child.

> *(Enter the Chorus from the direction of
> the camp, chanting in anapests.)*

CHORUS:
I have come in a hurry to meet you here, Hecuba,
slipping away from the tent of my master
where I've been allotted, assigned as a slave
driven here by the Greeks from the city of Ilion—
100   a war captive, hunted and taken at spearpoint.
The message I bring will not lighten your suffering;
no, I am bearing a weight of great sorrow.

In the Greeks' full assembly, it was resolved
(we have heard) that your daughter be given in sacrifice,

---

5. Helenus was a son of Priam and Hecuba who had prophetic abilities. He
was captured by the Greeks and told them what they must do to take Troy.
In *Andromache* (1294), Thetis predicts that he will marry Andromache.

6. Cassandra, a daughter of Hecuba and Priam, had prophetic abilities but
was cursed not to be believed, since she refused sexual favors to the god
Apollo. During the capture of Troy she was sexually assaulted by Ajax son
of Oïleus, but then taken as a concubine by the leader of the Greeks, King
Agamemnon of Mycenae.

slaughtered to placate Achilles. You know   105
he appeared on his tomb, in his armor of gold,
and his cry held the ships as they set out to sea,
as their sails filled with wind, swelling into the forestays:

"Where are you going, Danaans?[7] How could you
abandon my tomb here with no prize of honor?"   110

Then a great wave of conflict crashed down on the crowd;
the spear-bearing host of the Greeks was divided
with some of them saying, yes! offer the sacrifice
there at the tomb, and some speaking against.

Agamemnon stayed true to the bed of the prophetess; [8]   115
he was the one who promoted your interests;
the scions of Athens, the two sons of Theseus
making two speeches, were both of one mind:[9]
fresh blood should adorn the tomb of Achilles;
the bed of Cassandra should never take precedence   120
over Achilles and his mighty spear.

The discussion was heated; each faction felt strongly.
The two sides were more or less even, and then
the son of Laertes,[10] the brilliant, smooth-talking,
crowd-pleasing master of verbal embroidery,   125
made his appeal to the army: it wouldn't be
right to say no to the greatest of all

---

7. In the classical period, the Greeks called themselves "Hellenes," but in
Homer they have a variety of names, which tragedy also uses: "Danaans"
here, "Achaeans" at 214, "Argives" at 180. There is no difference in
meaning.

8. That is, Cassandra.

9. It was a problem for the Athenians that they were unimportant in the
Trojan War, and tragedies tend to make the Athenians more prominent
than the epic does. Menestheus, the Athenian leader in Homer's *Iliad,*
was an interloper—he was made ruler of Athens by Helen's brothers,
the Dioscuri (Spartans!), when Theseus was away. Because Theseus was
associated with the origins of the democracy, the Athenians followed the
later epics *Little Iliad* and *Sack of Troy* in making his sons Acamas and
Demophon their commanders at Troy. It is remarkable, though, that they
here play an unsympathetic role.

10. The son of Laertes is Odysseus.

the Danaans, and we should be willing to sacrifice
slaves for his sake—let no one of the perished
130   declare to Persephone, standing before her,[11]
that this is the way the Danaans ungraciously
treated Danaans who died for the Greeks
when they sailed off from Troy.

Odysseus will come here—he's already left—
135   to tear the young filly away from your breast
and haste her away from your elderly arms.[12]

But go to the temples, go to the altars!
Beg Agamemnon—take hold of his knees![vi]
Call on the heavenly gods, and the gods
dwelling under the earth.

140   If your prayers can prevail,
they'll keep you from losing your unhappy child;
if not, you must watch as the virgin falls forward
onto the tomb, and her blood stains it crimson,
flowing in lustrous black streams from her throat
145   encircled with gold.

HECUBA: *(Singing.)*

[Strophe]

Oh, unhappy me. What cry, what lament
what weeping can help an old woman,
unsaved, unsalved, enslaved?
Unbearable, unendurable.
150   Who defends me? What family, what city?
The old man is gone,
the children are gone.
I don't know which direction to step.
This way? That way? Where will I be safe?
155   What god, what divinity stands at my side?
O daughters of Troy, bearing tidings of pain,

---

11. Persephone is the Queen of the Underworld, wife of the god Hades.
12. The comparison of young girls to fawns, heifers (see 200 and 546), or fillies was by this time conventional.

you have borne so much pain, you've destroyed me,
                              destroyed me.
The daylight no longer means anything to me.
My life means nothing now.

This way, poor old foot. Come on, carry an old woman   160
to this homestead, this tent.

    (Hecuba approaches the tent.)

O daughter, O child
of a most unfortunate
mother, come out now,
come out of the house,   165
come hear your mother's voice.

Oh my child.[vii]

    (Enter Polyxena from the tent, singing.)

POLYXENA:
Mother, why are you shouting?
What next? What's the news?
Mother, you've startled me out of the house   170
like a terrified bird.

HECUBA:
Alas, my child.

POLYXENA:
What is this unholy prelude to sorrow?

HECUBA:
Ah. Your life.

POLYXENA:
Speak out! Please, conceal it no longer.   175
I'm afraid, I'm afraid, Mother.
Why are you weeping?

HECUBA:
My child, O child of an unhappy mother . . .

POLYXENA:
What are you telling me?

HECUBA:
180 The Argives' consensus impels them
to slaughter you upon the tomb
of Peleus' son.

POLYXENA:
Alas, Mother. What are you saying?
Tell me of this sorrow, Mother;
185 tell me this unenviable tale.

HECUBA:
My child, the report I bring is unholy;
the Argives are resolved, their vote is cast
concerning your fate.

POLYXENA:

[Antistrophe][viii]

O Mother, what terrible woes you've endured;
190 you've suffered a lifetime of anguish.
Some god has once again
afflicted you with unspeakable,
most detestable outrage. No longer,
no longer will I,
195 your child, enslaved
and unsalved, be beside you, poor thing,
in your old age. You will see me torn
right out of your arms, like a cub that's been raised
away in the mountains—poor Mother, poor me—
200 like a heifer, my throat cut, and hurled down to Hades;
I'll lie underground with the dead in the darkness
beneath the earth, forlorn.

O Mother, what ruin, what misfortune oppresses you.
It's for you that I sing
205 my tearful lament.
For myself I shed no tears—
not for this outrage,

this insult. I've found
a better fate, my death.

CHORUS: .
  Look: here comes Odysseus, in quite a rush;   210
  He'll tell you, Hecuba, what will be next.[ix]

  (Enter Odysseus from the direction of the camp.)

ODYSSEUS:
  Woman, I think you know the army's mind
  and what has been decreed. Still, I will tell you.
  The Achaeans have resolved to sacrifice
  Polyxena, your daughter, at the site   215
  of Achilles' lofty burial mound and grave.
  They designated me to be her convoy
  and to escort her there. The appointed priest
  presiding at the sacrificial rite
  will be Achilles' son. You are aware   220
  of how you must conduct yourself: don't think
  your hands' and arms' strength can contend with mine;
  don't make me have to drag you off by force.
  Recognize where your safety lies; acknowledge
  your present troubles. The better part of wisdom   225
  is to keep your thoughts in line, even in troubles.

HECUBA:
  Ah. Here's a contest—and the stakes are high—
  suffused with groans, and not devoid of tears.
  It's clear now that I did not meet my death
  back where I should have. Zeus did not destroy me;   230
  he keeps me going so that I may see
  still greater sorrows added to my sorrows.

  If it's allowed for servants to ask questions
  that cause no pain, and do not sting the heart
  of free men, then it's right that you should speak   235
  and we, the questioners, should listen to you.

ODYSSEUS:
  It is allowed; ask. I don't begrudge the time.

HECUBA:
　　You know when you came to Ilion, a spy,[13]
　　disguised in shabby clothes, with drops of blood
240　　trickling from your eyes down to your jaw?

ODYSSEUS:
　　Yes, I know. It touched my inmost heart.

HECUBA:
　　And Helen knew you, and told only me?

ODYSSEUS:
　　I remember. I was in great danger.

HECUBA:
　　You were humbled, and took hold of my knees?

ODYSSEUS:
245　　I gripped your robe so hard my hand went dead.

HECUBA:
　　Well, then. I saved you, and sent you from our land?

ODYSSEUS:
　　Because of that, I live to see this daylight.

HECUBA:
　　What did you say, then, when you were my slave?

ODYSSEUS:
　　The words came easily. I didn't want to die.

HECUBA:
250　　Well, aren't you ashamed, then, of these counsels,
　　you, whom I treated just as you describe,

---

13. In Homer's *Odyssey,* Helen tells the story of how Odysseus came to
Troy as a spy and how she recognized him but did not give him away.
Euripides has freely invented Hecuba's role in this story and thus makes
Odysseus indebted to her.

and now, instead of showing any kindness,
intend to do us all the harm you can?
You're an ungracious breed, you demagogues,
lusting for acclaim. Oh, I want nothing   255
to do with you. You don't care if you hurt
a friend or loved one, if your words find favor
with the masses.
                    Tell me, now: how do you figure
that this is something clever, this decree
to put a child to death? Were you compelled   260
to slaughter a human victim at the tomb
where cattle sacrifice would be more proper?
Perhaps Achilles wants his just revenge:
murder, to strike back at murderers.
But this girl hasn't done him any harm!ˣ   265
Or, if a beautiful captive has to die,
don't look to us for the choicest offering:
Tyndareos' daughter has the loveliest form¹⁴
and her injustice outweighs ours. In fact,
justice is my main contention here.   270
Listen: you must pay me back; I'll tell you
what I'm asking in return. As you admit,
you once fell at my feet and took my hand,
and touched the cheek of this old woman. Now

(Hecuba kneels and touches Odysseus' hand and cheek.)

I'm touching yours, I am your suppliant,   275
I'm begging for repayment; please, be gracious.ˣⁱ
Please, don't drag my child from my arms,
don't kill her. Enough have died already.
She's my escape from sorrows, my delight,
my coolness, my relief from many things,   280
my city and my nurse, my staff, my guide.

Those with power should stay within their limits;
the fortunate should realize their joy
may not go on forever. Look at me:
I'm not what I once was; a single day   285
divested me of all the wealth I had.

---

14. Tyndareos' daughter is Helen.

I beg you by your beard, show reverence
and pity. Go to the Achaean army,
and change their minds; tell them that killing women
290   will stir up grudges; when you had the chance,
before, when you had dragged them from the altars,
you didn't kill them—you had pity. Tell them
Greek law regarding bloodshed is the same
for free men and for slaves.[15] And your prestige,
295   even if you don't speak well, will strengthen
your appeal. The identical argument
can have a very different effect
depending on the speaker's reputation.

CHORUS:
No one could have such a brutal nature
300   that he could hear your cries, your lingering wail
of lamentation, and not shed a tear.

ODYSSEUS:
Hecuba, take a lesson from me now:
don't hate the man who speaks well, just because
your mind is fuming with rage. I am prepared
305   to save your life, and I stand by my statement.
You treated me kindly; I was fortunate.
But I will not take back the proposition
I made to the assembly: now that Troy
is taken, we should offer to the army's
310   greatest man the sacrifice he asks for:
your child.
                  So many cities are undone
by this mistake: the noble man, the eager
benefactor, gets no more reward
than lesser men. Achilles is deserving
315   of every honor, woman: he has died
a most glorious death for Hellas, for his country.

---

15. This is roughly true; killing a slave incurred ritual pollution just as killing a free person did. However, since only a relative of a murder victim could prosecute, and the master was the slave's only legal family, nobody would have standing to prosecute a man who killed his own slave.

Well, isn't it shameful to treat him as a friend
while he's alive, but not when he has perished?
What, then, will people say, if there's another
marshaling of troops, another contest   320
against the enemy? Will we fight then? Or
will we simply be in love with our survival,
since, as we've seen, the dead receive no honor?
Look: for my part, I don't ask for much
while I'm alive—enough to make it through   325
from one day to the next. But I would want
a tomb with some distinction, one that shows
long-lasting gratitude for what I've done.

And as for all your pitiful suffering—
I've heard you out, now you listen to me—   330
we have old women whose sheer wretchedness
outweighs yours, and old men, too, and brides
whose husbands, excellent young men, lie dead here,
the dust of Ida covering their bodies.
You must endure what happens.
                      Our Greek custom   335
of honoring the noble may well strike you
as idiotic. All right, then: we're fools.
You barbarians go right on ahead
not treating friends as friends, not valuing
those who die with glory. Greece will have   340
good fortune, and *your* fates will match your counsels.[xii]

CHORUS:
   Ah. Slavery is an evil; defeated by violence
   slaves endure what they should never have to.

HECUBA:
   My words are wasted, flung up to the sky
   and gone. My child, I can't prevent your murder.   345
   But you, if you have more strength than your mother,
   go on, and like a nightingale, pour
   your voice out, every note, to save your life.
   Throw yourself pitifully at Odysseus' knee
   and make your appeal on these grounds: he himself   350
   has children. He may pity your hard fortune.

POLYXENA:

Odysseus, I see that you are hiding
your right hand underneath your cloak, and turning
your face away, so I can't touch your beard.[16]
You're off the hook; don't worry. I refuse
to call on Zeus, Protector of Suppliants.
Since I'm compelled, I'll follow you, and also
since death is what I want. If I resist
I'll be no good, in love with mere survival.
Why should I live? My father was the lord
of all the Phrygians.[17] That was my starting point.
Then, I was raised on promises and hopes
of royal marriage, and keen rivalry
to see whose hearth and home I would belong to.
Unlucky me—I was the princess once,
first among the women of Ida, admired
among the maidens, equal to the gods
in all but one respect: mortality.

And now I am a slave. The name, to start with—
so unfamiliar!—makes me long for death.
And then, I might get cruel-minded masters;
whoever pays for me with silver—me,
sister of Hector, and of many others!—
will give me orders, tell me that I must
make bread, and sweep the house, and do my weaving,
spending painful days under compulsion.
Some paid-for slave from somewhere will defile
my bed, which was prestigious once, considered
a prize for rulers.   No! I'm free to close
my eyes forever, turn from this day's light,
give my body to Hades. Go ahead,

---

16. In the ritual of supplication, the supplicator touched the chin and
kissed the hand of the person supplicated, thereby asking for protection in
the name of Zeus. Odysseus' gesture prevents Polyxena from performing
the ritual.

17. Phrygia was a kingdom in west-central Anatolia; in tragedy it is often
identified with Troy. Phrygia had gold mines and was the legendary home
of King Midas.

Odysseus, lead me away now, and destroy me.
I have no hope of any future joy.
Mother, please don't say or do a thing
to stop me. You should want, as much as I do,   385
for me to die before submitting myself
to shameful humiliation, far beneath
our family's level of distinction. Someone
who's not familiar with the taste of troubles
may wear the yoke, but it will hurt his neck.   390
Such a person would be more fortunate
dead than alive. A base life is a hardship.

CHORUS:
Nobility is clearly stamped; the sign
is wondrous and impressive—all the more so
for those who prove they're worthy of distinction.   395

HECUBA:
You've spoken beautifully, child, but there is grief
beneath the beauty.
                        Odysseus, if you really
must show your gratitude to Peleus' son
in order to avoid blame, don't kill *her!*
Lead *me* to the pyre of Achilles   400
and stab me; don't restrain your hand. You know
that I bore Paris, the one who, with his arrows,
destroyed the son of Thetis.[18]

ODYSSEUS:
                        Achilles' ghost
asked for *her* death, old woman, not for yours.

HECUBA:
All right—then murder me together with her;   405
pour a double blood-offering to the earth
and to the corpse who's asking for this drink.

---

18. Thetis, a sea goddess, was Achilles' mother.

ODYSSEUS:
Your girl's death is enough; no need for more.
If only hers were not compulsory.

HECUBA:
410   I must die together with my daughter.

ODYSSEUS:
I didn't realize you were my master.

HECUBA:
I'll cling to her like ivy to an oak.

ODYSSEUS:
Not if you obey those who are wiser.

HECUBA:
I will not willingly let go of this child.

ODYSSEUS:
415   Nor will I go away and leave her here.

POLYXENA:
Mother, listen to me. And you, son of Laertes,
ease up on her a little: it's natural
for her to fume with rage. Oh, Mother, poor thing,
don't fight this battle; they're the ones in power.
420   Do you want to fall to the ground, cast down by force?
They'll lacerate your ancient skin; you'll lose
your dignity; some youthful arm will grab you
and drag you off; you'll suffer all these things.
No, Mother—it would be unworthy of you.

425   O my dearest, give me your sweet hand,
come here and place your cheek against my cheek,
for after this, I never will again
see the sun's great circle, and its blaze.[xiii]
These are the final words I'll speak to you.
430   I'm going now, Mother, I'm going down below.

HECUBA:
I pity you, child. Oh, I am so wretched.

POLYXENA:
There in Hades I'll lie, apart from you.

HECUBA:
What will I do? Oh, where will my life end?

POLYXENA:
I'll die a slave, though my father was a free man.

HECUBA:
O daughter, I shall live on as a slave.   435

POLYXENA:
I should have had a bridegroom and a wedding.[xiv]

HECUBA:
My fifty children, gone. I'm left with nothing.

POLYXENA:
What shall I say to Hector, or your husband?

HECUBA:
Tell them I am the most wretched of all women.

POLYXENA:
O motherly breasts, that sweetly nurtured me!   440

HECUBA:
O daughter, what wretched misfortune to die young!

POLYXENA:
Mother who bore me, farewell. Farewell, Cassandra . . .

HECUBA:
Others may fare well, but I cannot.

POLYXENA:
. . . and Polydorus, my brother, in horse-loving Thrace.

HECUBA:
If he lives—but I don't believe it. My misfortune is total.   445

POLYXENA:
 He lives! He'll close your eyes when you have died.

HECUBA:
 I have died already from sorrow, before my death.

POLYXENA:
 Odysseus, drape this robe around my head
 and lead me away. My mother's lament has melted
450 my heart already, before my slaughter, and I
 am melting her with my crying.
                              O light of day,
 I speak your name, but all I have left of you
 is one short moment, as I traverse the distance
 from here to the sword's blade and Achilles' pyre.

HECUBA:
455 Oh, I can't—my limbs won't hold me up.
 O daughter, clasp your mother, extend your arm,
 give me your hand, don't leave me childless.
                                        My friends,
 I am destroyed. If only I could see
 the Laconian sister of the Dioscuri,[19]
460 Helen, destroyed this way. Her lovely eyes
 brought hellish[xv] ruin to all of Troy's good fortune.

 *(Odysseus leads Polyxena away toward the
 camp. Hecuba falls to the ground in despair.)*

CHORUS:

                       [Strophe 1]

 Breeze, ocean[xvi] breeze,
 you spirit the oceangoing barks away
 far over the deep sea waves;
465 now where will you lead unhappy me?
 Whose house will I belong to
 as slave and possession?

---

19. The Dioscuri, Castor and Polydeuces, demigods who rescued sailors,
were Helen's brothers.

Will I arrive at a harbor in Dorian country
or come to the land of Phthia[20]
where father Apidanus, so they say,   470
enriches the plain with the loveliest of streams?

[Antistrophe 1]

Salt-sweeping oar,
Will you send me to an island, where I'll spend
a pitiful life indoors?
Perhaps I'll reside where Leto grasped   475
the saplings of the date palm—[21]
the first in the world—and
bay laurel, cherished memento and sacred emblem
of birth pangs for Zeus' children.
Will I sing with the Delian girls in praise   480
of Artemis' bow and her diadem of gold?

[Strophe 2]

Or perhaps in Pallas' city
I'll fashion on her saffron robe
an intricate image
woven in flower tones: 485
the fillies as they're yoked
to Athena's lovely chariot,
or the race of Titans[xvii]
as Zeus, son of Cronus, lays them to rest
with his fire-flanked bolt of lightning.[22]   490

---

20. Phthia, the homeland of Achilles in northern Greece, was in southeast Thessaly; the river Apidanus flows northwest through Thessaly and into the Peneus. Euripides often celebrates places outside Athens, especially those where the plays were likely to be read or produced, such as Thessaly and Sicily.

21. Leto gave birth to Apollo and Artemis under the sacred palm tree of Delos.

22. They are imagining that they will work on the robe given to the statue of Athena at the Panathenaea. This work was actually performed not by slaves but by aristocratic women.

[Antistrophe 2]

O my children, O my parents,
O homeland—broken, smoldering wreck!
O spear-captive city
choking on Argive smoke,
495   I'll change my name to "slave,"
I'll trade Asia for a foreign land
and I'll leave the chambers
of Hades behind, to take in exchange
a new shelter, a home in Europe.

(Enter Talthybius from the camp.)[23]

TALTHYBIUS:
500   Daughters of Troy, where might I find the one
who once was Lady of Ilion, Hecuba?

CHORUS:
Talthybius, she's right here on the ground,
wrapped in her robes and lying on her back.

TALTHYBIUS:
O Zeus, what can I say? Do you watch over
505   mankind, or is that just a useless rumor[xviii]
and Fortune is our only overseer?
Isn't this woman the Lady of golden Phrygia,
Isn't she wife of Priam, with all his riches?
And now her city is utterly razed by the spear
510   and she herself is lying on the ground,
an elderly slave, childless, miserable,
rubbing dust into her hair. Oh god.
I'm old myself, but I would sooner die
than meet with shameful fortune. Raise yourself,
515   poor miserable woman; get off the ground,
lift up your body and your old white head!

(Talthybius attempts to lift Hecuba to her feet.)

---

23. Talthybius, the herald of Agamemnon or of the Greek army as a whole, was a familiar character in plays set in Troy.

HECUBA:
Stop! Why are you prodding me? Leave me alone
to lie here in my pain, whoever you are.

TALTHYBIUS:
I'm Talthybius, in the Danaans' service.
I've come for you because Agamemnon sent me.　　　520

HECUBA:
Most welcome visitor! Have the Greeks resolved
to slaughter me as well upon the grave?
I'd love that—lead the way. Let's not waste time.

TALTHYBIUS:
Your daughter is dead. I've come to find you, ma'am,
so you can bury her. I have been sent　　　525
by Atreus' sons[24] and the Achaean people.

HECUBA:
Oh no, what are you saying? You're not here
to lead me to my death, but only to break
my heart with sorrow?
　　　　　　　　　My child, you are destroyed,
torn from your mother, and I'm alone without you.　　　530

Did the army show any reverence when they killed her?
Or did you all approach this dreadful thing
as if you were putting an enemy to death?
Old man, let's hear the whole unwelcome story.

TALTHYBIUS:
You're asking me to reap a double profit　　　535
of tears: I wept for pity when she died
there at the grave, and now as I recount
these sorrows, once again my eyes are wet.

The entire crowd was gathered at the tomb—
the full assembly of the Achaean army—　　　540
to witness your girl's sacrifice. The child

---

24. Agamemnon and Menelaus.

of Achilles took Polyxena by the hand
and stood her at the top of the burial mound.
I was nearby. A hand-picked group of men,
545   the choicest youths of the Achaeans, followed
in case your frisky heifer needed restraining.
Achilles' child took the golden cup
in both his hands—it was completely full—
then raised it with one hand as a libation
550   to his dead father. He gave me the sign
to silence the entire Achaean army.
I took my stand among them and announced:
"Silence, Achaeans! Let every man of you
be silent now!" I quieted the crowd;
555   they stood there like a calm and windless sea.
He spoke: "My father, son of Peleus,
receive now this libation, which I make
to attract and to enchant the dead! Come here
that you may drink this maiden's pure black blood,
560   which is your gift from me and from the army.
Look favorably on us now; release
our sterns, undo the mooring cables; grant
a favorable journey home from Troy—
may we all reach our fatherlands in safety."

565   Thus he spoke, and all the army prayed.
And then he took the handle of his dagger
inlaid with gold, and drew it from its sheath
and nodded to the army's finest youths
that they should take the virgin. When she saw this,
570   she said these words: "O Argives, ravagers
of my city, I die willingly.
Let no one lay a hand upon my skin.
I'm fearless; I will offer up my throat,
but, by the gods, I want to die in freedom.
575   I am a princess; I would be ashamed
to have the name of 'slave' among the dead."

A murmur rose from the people, like the sound
of waves on pebbles, and Lord Agamemnon
told the young men to release the virgin.[xix]
580   When she had heard this order from their master
she took her robe and tore it from the shoulder

to the midriff, stopping at her navel, showing
her breasts—her chest was very beautiful,
just like a statue—then she dropped her knee
onto the earth, and spoke these words of endurance,   585
the bravest I have ever heard: "Young man,
look at me: if you intend to strike
my breast, then strike here; if you want my neck
then here it is. I'm ready."
                              Out of pity
for the girl, he was both willing and unwilling.   590
His iron cut right through the passageway
through which her breath flowed. Blood poured out in streams.
Even as she died, she had the foresight
to fall without displaying anything
that should be hidden from the eyes of men.   595
Once she'd received the sacrificial deathblow
and breathed her last, the Argives went to work:
some carried leaves in their hands, to strew her body;[25]
others carried pine logs for her pyre,
filling in the spaces. Anyone   600
who wasn't carrying something was rebuked:
"Are you just standing there? You're empty-handed?
You're the worst! Go now, and bring a gift—
a robe, some jewelry—for this young woman
who was so very fearless, and whose soul   605
was greatest of all."
                    As I speak these words
about the way your daughter died, I regard you
as blessed beyond all others in your children,
and yet the most unfortunate of women.

CHORUS:
Compelled by the gods, a dreadful, seething pain   610
has touched my city and the sons of Priam.

HECUBA:
O daughter, I don't know which way to look,

---

25. It was customary to throw leaves over victorious athletes, and possibly
over bridal couples.

which sorrow to address—there are so many.
If I take hold of one, another grief,
615   trouble on top of trouble, calls me away.
I couldn't wipe your suffering from my mind,
and yet I cannot mourn excessively
when I hear how nobly you acted.
                                        Well, isn't it strange
that crops can flourish on inferior land
620   if the gods provide exactly what is needed,
and decent land, if anything goes wrong,
bears lesser fruit—it's different, though, with people:
a malicious man is never anything but
malicious, and the noble are always noble;
625   disaster can't erase their decency.
What makes the difference: birth, or upbringing?
Being raised well certainly can teach
nobility, and whoever learns that lesson
can learn what's shameful, by comparison.

630   So much for that. My mind shoots useless arrows.

         (To Talthybius)

You: go and tell the Argives not to touch
my child, and keep the crowd away from her.
An army of such size might let the crowd
run riot. Sailors cannot be controlled;
635   they're worse than wildfire. Any man who won't
commit a crime is branded as a coward.

         *(Exit Talthybius to the camp. Hecuba
         addresses her Servant.)*

You, my longtime servant, take this vessel:
go dip it in the ocean, fill it up
with seawater, and bring it back to me
640   so I can give my child her final bath—
this bride who's no bride, virgin who's no virgin—
and lay her out in a manner worthy—how?
I couldn't. I will have to—what else is there?—
gather up jewelry from the captive women
645   who dwell beside me here within this tent;

They might have some adornments they have stolen
from their own homes, and snuck past our new masters.

O sheltering houses! Homes once fortunate!

(Exit Servant with vessel, toward the seashore.)

O Priam, you were richest in possessions
and blessed beyond all others in your children;   650
you and I, their mother, an old woman—
we've come to nothing, stripped of all defiance.
What happens to our self-importance now?
Will anyone take pride in his rich home
or how the city holds his name in honor?   655
All that means nothing—the mind's useless counsels,
the tongue's vain boasts. Call that man prosperous
who makes it through each day without some shock.

(Exit Hecuba and attendant into Agamemnon's tent.)

CHORUS:

[Strophe]

Disaster had to happen,
pain had to stake its claim on me, from the moment   660
fir trees on Ida were felled
so Paris could sail on the deep salt waves of the sea
for the bedroom of Helen,
the most beautiful woman
whom Helios touches   665
with his golden beams.

[Antistrophe]

Our hardships, and compulsion—
stronger still than our struggles—circle to meet us.
One person's crazy misstep
destroyed everyone in the land where Simoïs flows.[26]   670
When the herdsman on Ida

---

26. Simoïs is the less important of the two rivers of the Troad in the *Iliad* (Scamander is the greater).

was the judge[27] in that conflict
among three divine ones
his decree unleashed

[Epode]

675   disaster, death at spearpoint, outrage in my halls.
And some Laconian girl, beside the rolling Eurotas,[28]
weeps and groans in her home, and a mother somewhere
strikes her gray head, tears her cheeks with her nails till
                                                     they bleed,
to mourn her dead children.

*(Enter the Servant from the seashore, with two
attendants carrying a covered body.)*[29]

SERVANT:
680   Women, where is Hecuba the wretched?
No man or woman born surpasses her
in sorrows—she has clearly won the prize.ˣˣ

CHORUS:
What, more bad news? Your poor tongue shrieks ill tidings?
These grim announcements never take a rest.

SERVANT:
685   I bring this painful news for Hecuba.
Good tidings are not always possible.

(Enter Hecuba from the tent.)

CHORUS:
Look: she's here, emerging from her home
exactly when she's needed, to hear your words.

---

27. The reference is to the Judgment of Paris.

28. The Eurotas River flows through Sparta. It is striking that the Chorus
here imagine also the suffering of the women on the other side.

29. The body of Polydorus is completely covered, so that even the sex of
the corpse is not recognizable, although the cloth is obviously not Greek.

SERVANT:
    Poor woman, enduring more than I can say,
    you exist no longer, though you see the daylight.   690
    You have no city, no husband, no child. You're crushed.

HECUBA:
    You've told me nothing new. Don't throw these words
    in my face; I know already. Tell me, now:
    why are you bringing me Polyxena's body?
    I heard that every Achaean hand was busy   695
    with her burial.

SERVANT:
                        She doesn't know, she hasn't grasped
    This new pain. She laments Polyxena.

HECUBA:
    Oh, poor me. Don't tell me it's Cassandra
    you're carrying, the prophet, the bacchante![30]

SERVANT:
    She lives—don't wail for her sake. Save your groans   700
    for him. This is the one who died. Look, now,

    (The attendants uncover Polydorus' corpse.)

    are you stunned? Is this beyond belief?

HECUBA:
    Alas. I see Polydorus; he's dead—my child,
    the one the Thracian was keeping safe at home.
    I am destroyed. Ah! I exist no longer.   705

        *(In the following exchange, Hecuba for the most
        part sings, and the Chorus and Servant speak.)*

---

30. Euripides uses the language of Dionysiac madness ("bacchante")
very freely for psychic disturbance, here for Cassandra's fits of prophetic
inspiration.

> O child, O my child,
> now is the time for wailing,
> crying the bacchic measure!
> Just now I have realized
710 these evils, this vengeful Curse!

CHORUS:
You understand the ruin your child has come to?

HECUBA:
This latest shock—it's unbelievable.[xxi]

> One sorrow stalks the next;
> never will I be free
715 of my groans, my tears!

CHORUS:
Our suffering is terrible, poor woman.

HECUBA:
> O child, O my child,
> how did you die? What doom
> took you from your poor mother?
720 What fate laid you low?
> Whose hand dealt the blow?

SERVANT:
I do not know. I found him on the seashore.

HECUBA:
Was he cast up there by the waves, or was it
a bloody spear that felled him on the spot
725 there on the glassy sand?

SERVANT:
A sea wave carried him and cast him forth.

HECUBA:
> Alas, oh alas,
> I now understand
> the vision I saw in the night,
730 the ghost with black wings! I saw

a vision of you, my child,
no longer living in Zeus's daylight.

CHORUS:
Who killed him? Did your dream reveal that?

HECUBA:
It was my host, my guest-friend,
the horseman of Thrace!   735
His old father sent him
to live there, in secret!

CHORUS:
What are you saying? He killed him for his gold?

HECUBA:
This is unspeakable.
Oh, I am more than stunned.   740
This is unholy, this is unbearable.
Where is the justice, where
is the bond between guest-friends?
O you accursèd man,
showing no pity, you   745
sheared through this child's skin,
hacked at his limbs with an iron dagger!

CHORUS:
Poor thing, some cruel god has given you
more hardship than any other living person.
But look, I see someone—it's Agamemnon,   750
your master. Let's be quiet now, my friends.

        (Enter Agamemnon from the camp.)

AGAMEMNON:
Hecuba, why the delay? Why haven't you come
to bury your child? We have observed the terms
Talthybius announced: no Argive man
may touch the girl. We have left her alone;   755
we haven't laid a finger on her. But you
are taking your time to come, and I'm amazed.

I've come to get you. Everything there has been
well taken care of—that is, if anything
about this can be called "well done."
760   Hold on—
who is this man I see beside the tent?
He's dead—a Trojan. I know he's not an Argive;
the robes enfolding him announce that clearly.

*(In the following dialogue, Hecuba's
back is turned to Agamemnon.)*

HECUBA:
    Unhappy creature—myself, that is. Hecuba,
765   what shall I do? Fall at Agamemnon's feet,
    clasp his knees, or bear these sorrows in silence?

AGAMEMNON:
    Why won't you face me? Why do you lament
    with your back turned? What happened? Who is this man?

HECUBA:
    But I'm his slave, his wartime foe. He might
770   push me away from his knees, increase my pain . . .

AGAMEMNON:
    Listen—I'm not a prophet. If I can't hear you
    then I can't know the path your counsels follow.

HECUBA:
    Then again, am I jumping to conclusions?
    Perhaps he's not my enemy after all.

AGAMEMNON:
775   If you intend for me to know nothing about this,
    then fine—nothing. I don't want to hear.

HECUBA:
    I couldn't avenge my children without this man.
    Why agonize? I am compelled to show
    daring in this matter, whether or not
    it does me any good.

*(Hecuba turns, kneels, and touches
Agamemnon's hand and cheek.)*[xxii]

O Agamemnon,   780
I beg you by your knees and by your beard,
and by your right hand, which is blessed by fortune.

AGAMEMNON:
What are you after? Do you want to live
in freedom? You could easily attain that.[31]

HECUBA:
No! If I can only have revenge,   785
I'm willing to live my whole life as a slave.

AGAMEMNON:
Then what do you need me to help you with?

HECUBA:
It isn't what you think, my lord. Do you see
this corpse here? It's for him I shed my tears.

AGAMEMNON:
I see him. But I still don't understand.   790

HECUBA:
I carried him within my womb; I bore him.

AGAMEMNON:
Poor thing—this man is one of your children, then?

HECUBA:
Not one of those who died defending Troy.

AGAMEMNON:
What? Is there any other child you bore?

HECUBA:
Yes—for nothing, so it seems. That's him.   795

---

31. Remarkably, Agamemnon seems ready to manumit Hecuba
immediately.

AGAMEMNON:
Where was he when the city was destroyed?

HECUBA:
His father sent him away, terrified he'd die.

AGAMEMNON:
Just him, out of them all? Where did he send him?

HECUBA:
To this place here—the place where we found him dead.

AGAMEMNON:
800   To Polymestor, the man who rules this land?

HECUBA:
We sent him with gold—the outcome was most bitter.

AGAMEMNON:
He's dead—by what fate? Whose hand dealt the blow?

HECUBA:
Who else? His host destroyed him—our Thracian friend.

AGAMEMNON:
You poor thing. He was in love with the gold, no doubt?

HECUBA:
805   Something like that. He learned of Troy's disaster.

AGAMEMNON:
And where did you find him? Or, who brought his corpse?

HECUBA: *(Indicating the Servant.)*
This woman found his body on the beach.

AGAMEMNON:
Looking for him, or doing other work?

HECUBA:
She went for salt water, to bathe Polyxena.

AGAMEMNON:
His host, it seems, killed him and cast him out . . .　　　　810

HECUBA:
. . . to drift on the sea. His skin was slashed and torn.

AGAMEMNON:
Poor woman. Your hardships are beyond all measure.

HECUBA:
I am destroyed. There's nothing left to suffer.

AGAMEMNON:
Has a woman so unfortunate ever lived?

HECUBA:
Never—unless you speak of Fortune herself.　　　　　815

I'll tell you why I've fallen at your knee.
Listen: if you think the things I've suffered
accord with holiness, then never mind—
I'll make my peace with them. If not, you must
take vengeance on this most unholy host　　　　　　820
for me. He didn't fear the gods above
or those below the earth, when he committed
this most unholy deed.ˣˣⁱⁱⁱ
　　　　　　　　　　We are slaves
and weak, perhaps. The gods, however, are strong
and so is law, which rules them. By this law　　　　825
we believe the gods exist, and we distinguish
what's just and unjust in our lives.[32] If the law
appears before you and gets ripped to shreds—
if those who murder guests, or those who dare
to plunder what is sacred, don't come to justice—[33]　　830
then there's no equal treatment among men.

---

32. A strange passage: Hecuba (like Socrates) believes in a law superior to the gods. This law (or "custom"), by creating a visible order in the world, makes people believe in the gods.

33. Murdering guests and temple robbing are among the crimes the Greeks believed would be universally repugnant.

You must condemn these things. Show reverence
and pity me: stand back, and like a painter
direct your gaze on me and all my sorrows.
835   I was a ruler once; now I'm your slave.
I once had lovely children; now I'm childless,
deserted, an old woman with no city,
most wretched of all mortals.

> *(Agamemnon attempts to extricate himself
> from Hecuba's suppliant grasp.)*

                              Oh no, no—
where are you trying to go? Why slip away?
840   It seems that I will fail. Alas, poor me.

We mortals toil for knowledge, as we must,
and study every other subject—why, then,
do we neglect the one that rules mankind:
Persuasion? That's the one that we should master;
845   and we should pay good money to learn how
to get our way by winning arguments.[34]

How could anyone still hope for joy?
The children that were mine exist no longer,
and I myself am shamed, a captive woman;
850   it's over now. Smoke spirals over Troy.
Look (maybe there's no point in bringing up
Aphrodite; still, it will be said):[35]
My daughter, Phoebus' prophetess, who's called
Cassandra by the Phrygians, lies down
855   beside you when you take your rest. My lord,
how much will you esteem these nights of love?
For the sake of love's embraces in bed, will you
show gratitude to my daughter, and for her sake
to me? The deepest human gratitude
860   comes from the magic charm of night, and favors

---

34. Persuasion (rhetoric) was central to the curriculum of the contemporary sophists and certainly not neglected in the contemporary world.

35. Hecuba shows concern not about whether it is appropriate to bring
up Agamemnon's relationship with her daughter, but whether it is a useful
line of argument for her.

given in the dark. Just listen, now.
Do you see this dead man? If you treat him well
it's your own brother-in-law you're taking care of.[36]
One more thing—if only the arts of Daedalus[37]
or of some god could give a speaking voice   865
to my arms, my hands, my hair, my feet in motion,
so they could all together hold your knees,
bring every type of argument to bear,
and cry to you—O master, greatest light
to the Greeks, let me persuade you: lend your hand   870
to this old woman, even if she's nothing—[38]
still, take vengeance. A noble man serves justice,
and always, everywhere, will harm the wicked.

CHORUS:
It's truly wondrous what befalls mankind;
compulsion's laws determine everything,[xxiv]   875
making friends of the bitterest wartime foes
and turning well-wishers into enemies.

AGAMEMNON:
I do feel pity, Hecuba, for you,
your child, your misfortunes, and your suppliant hand.
I want that unholy host to come to justice,   880
as is right, and as the gods demand,
and—somehow, if there's any way—for you
to benefit, without the army thinking
that Cassandra's favors made me plan the murder
of the Thracian lord. For I must keep in mind—   885
a disturbing thought has occurred to me—the army
considers that man friendly, and the dead man
an enemy. If he is dear to you,[xxv]
so what? The army doesn't care about that.
Think about it, then. I'll help you out,   890

---

36. She speaks as if Agamemnon were married to Cassandra.

37. Daedalus, the mythical artisan, could make talking statues.

38. Hecuba fantasizes voices in her limbs and hair because she has no
other allies. She imagines what these other voices would say and so speaks
of herself in the third person.

your struggles will be mine, I'll run to your side—
but if the Achaeans will find fault with me
I won't run quite so fast.

HECUBA:

                              Ah. There is no one
alive who's really free. One man is a slave
895   to money, one to fortune; in the city
the mob's opinion and the written laws
stop men from following their inclinations.
But since you are afraid, and hold the crowd
in such regard, I'll set you free from fear.
900   If I should plan to harm the man who killed

                    (Indicating Polydorus' corpse.)

this man, then share the knowledge, not the deed.

If you hear any racket, if the Achaeans
should rush to help the Thracian gentleman
when he suffers just what he will suffer,
905   then stop them, but don't let on that you are doing
any favor to me. As for the rest, don't worry:
I will make things right.

AGAMEMNON:

                              What will you do?
Will you clutch a dagger in your withered hand
to kill the barbarian? Or will you use poison?
910   What help will you have, whose hand, what friends?

HECUBA: *(Indicating Agamemnon's tent.)*
This shelter hides a crowd of Trojan women.

AGAMEMNON:
You mean the captives, prey of the Greek army?

HECUBA:
With their help I'll avenge my children's murder.

AGAMEMNON:
And how will women overpower men?

HECUBA:
A mob that uses trickery has wondrous   915
force, not easy to withstand.

AGAMEMNON:
                    Yes, wondrous.
But you're women. What use is the female race?

HECUBA:
What—? Didn't women kill Aegyptus' sons
and every male on the isle of Lemnos?[39]

> *(Hecuba rises to her feet, abandoning
> the suppliant posture.)*

Proceed as follows: leave off this discussion,   920

> *(Indicating the Servant.)*

and give this woman safe conveyance, please,
through the army.

> *(To the Servant.)*

                    You, approach our Thracian
host, and tell him this: "The one who once
was Lady of Ilion, Hecuba, summons you.
It's urgent, for your sake no less than hers,   925
and for your sons'; they too must hear her words."

I ask you, Agamemnon, to delay
the burial of Polyxena, freshly slaughtered.
These two, side by side, shall be consumed
by a single flame, double heartbreak for their mother,   930
then covered up with earth, sister and brother.

---

39. The fifty daughters of Danaus were forced to marry their Egyptian
cousins; all but one killed their husbands on their wedding night. The
women of Lemnos failed to worship Aphrodite, who cursed them with a
bad smell. When their husbands took concubines from Thrace, the women
murdered all the men on the island, except that Hypsipyle spared her father
Thoas. These are traditional examples of extreme female violence and do
not ring auspiciously.

AGAMEMNON:

    So be it. If the army had the chance
    to sail now, I could never grant this favor.
    But as it is, some god withholds the winds
935   and we're compelled to wait, at rest, and watch
    for sailing weather.[40]
                  May this turn out well
    somehow. One thing that everyone agrees on
    and cares about, each person and each city,
    is that the bad should suffer, the decent prosper.

    (Exit Agamemnon and the Servant.)

CHORUS:

               [Strophe 1]

940   O my Ilion, O my fatherland,
    once it was said that you
    had never been taken; that is no longer
    true—you've been ravaged, trapped in fogbank of Greeks;
    their spears, their spears ripped the garland
945   of towers down from your brow,
    and they stained you, defiled you with smoke.
    How I pity you—the homeplace
    where I'll no longer set foot.

               [Antistrophe 1]

    My destruction struck in the dead of night:
950   after the banquet, sleep
    was spreading its sweetness over my eyelids;
    after the ritual offering, the singing, the dance,
    my husband lay in the bedroom—
    his pikestaff hung on its peg—
955   he was no longer keeping his watch
    as the sailors made their way toward
    Ilion, stepping ashore.[xxvi]

---

40. This mention of delaying winds could imply that the gods are helping
Hecuba achieve her vengeance.

[Strophe 2]

I was fixing my hair
and binding it up in a headband, while gazing
at the endless gleams of light in my golden mirror   960
as I got ready to fall into bed.
But I heard a noise, and the streets of my city, Troy,
rang out with this charge: "When, O children of the Greeks,
when will you ravage Ilion's hilltop fortress
and return to your homes?"   965

[Antistrophe 2]

I abandoned love's bed
(in only my robe, like a Dorian maiden)[41]
and I went to holy Artemis, sat before her
but I got nowhere; poor me, I was led
to the briny sea, after watching my husband die;   970
I cast a glance back at my city as the ship
sped me away from Ilion, set off homeward,
and the pain was too much—

[Epode]

I cursed Helen, the Zeus-born twins' sister,
and Paris the Parasite, Paris the Terror,[xxvii]   975
since I was destroyed, driven out of my home
by that marriage—no marriage, but misery,
bred by some vengeful Curse. May the briny sea
never carry her back; may she never arrive
at her father's home.   980

> (Enter Polymestor from the direction of the camp
> with his two sons, attendants, and the Servant.
> Polymestor wears woven robes of Thracian
> design and carries two javelins. Hecuba bows her
> head to avoid eye contact with Polymestor.)

---

41. The Athenians contrasted the usual dress of Athenian women with
the allegedly skimpy "Dorian [='Spartan'] dress," the single peplos. Here
it is, in effect, a nightgown, but the women of the Chorus are probably still
wearing it. The peplos was held at the shoulder by long pins or brooches,
which the women use as weapons later.

POLYMESTOR:
O Priam, most beloved of all men!
And you, my most beloved Hecuba,
I weep at the sight of you, and of your city,
and of your child, who died so recently.

Ah.
985 Nothing can be trusted; neither prestige
nor hope of further happiness when life
is going well. The gods just mix things up,
create disturbances, so we'll revere them,
not knowing any better. But what's the point
990 of lamenting this? It doesn't clear the way
for any lessening of future sorrows.

I hope that you won't blame me for not coming
earlier. In fact, I was away
when you arrived here; I was visiting
995 the interior of Thrace. Once I'd returned,
I was setting out from home, when this woman here,
your slave, fell in with me, and spoke your message.
I heard it, and I'm here now.

HECUBA:
                                    Polymestor,
I'd be ashamed to meet your gaze directly
1000 in my present sorry state. You knew me when
my fortunes were much greater; reverence
will not permit me to look you in the eye
under these circumstances—you see my fate.
Don't take it as a sign of disrespect[xxviii]
1005 that a woman won't look directly at a man.

POLYMESTOR:
Not at all—it's no wonder, really.
But what do you need? Why did you send for me?

HECUBA:
There's something private I would like to say
to you and your children. Please tell your attendants
1010 to leave, and keep their distance from these quarters.

POLYMESTOR: *(To his attendants.)*
You may go.

(Exit the attendants. Polymestor addresses Hecuba.)

There: they've deserted us,
but there's no danger; you're my friend, and so is
the Achaean army. You must tell me, now:
how should a friend assist a friend who's stuck
in such a joyless state? I'm here to help you.   1015

HECUBA:
First, answer me: the child in your home
whom you received from his father's hand and mine,
Polydorus: is he alive? I need to know this.

POLYMESTOR:
Yes, yes! Where he's concerned, you have good fortune.

HECUBA:
Most beloved man! Well spoken, worthy of you.   1020

POLYMESTOR:
What else do you desire to learn from me?

HECUBA:
Does he think of me at all—the mother who bore him?

POLYMESTOR:
Yes; he was trying to come to you in secret.

HECUBA:
And the gold he brought from Troy—is it still safe?

POLYMESTOR:
It's safe. It's being guarded in my house.   1025

HECUBA:
Keep it safe, then. Don't desire what's not yours.

POLYMESTOR:
No, no! May I profit from what's mine already.

HECUBA:
    All right. Do you know what it is I want to tell you?

POLYMESTOR:
    No, I don't. You'll have to spell it out.

HECUBA:
1030   There's—O dear friend, beloved now as always . . .

POLYMESTOR:
    What? What should we know, my sons and I?

HECUBA:
    . . . ancient caverns, where Priam's gold is hidden.

POLYMESTOR:
    That's what you want to tell your son about?

HECUBA:
    Yes, yes—through you, since you're a pious man.

POLYMESTOR:
1035   Why is it that my children must be present?

HECUBA:
    If you should die, it's better that they know.

POLYMESTOR:
    You've spoken well. Of course, this way is wiser.

HECUBA:
    All right. Do you know the dwelling of Trojan Athena?[42]

POLYMESTOR:
    That's where the gold is? What marks the place, exactly?

---

42. Although Athena is vehemently anti-Trojan in the *Iliad,* she has a temple on the acropolis of Troy. The Parthenon was in effect the Athenian treasury, so Euripides' audience would find it plausible to say that the gold was hidden under the protection of Athena's temple.

HECUBA:
There's a black stone that juts out from the ground.   1040

POLYMESTOR:
Yes. Is there anything else you'd like to tell me?

HECUBA:
I brought some valuables—can you keep them safe?

POLYMESTOR:
Where do you have them? Hidden in your robes?xxix

HECUBA: *(Indicating Agamemnon's tent.)*
They're safe in this dwelling, packed in with the spoils.

POLYMESTOR:
Where? The Achaeans' ships are all around here.   1045

HECUBA:
The captive women have a private dwelling.

POLYMESTOR:
It's safe inside? Deserted of all men?

HECUBA:
There's no Achaean man inside—just women.
Get in the house. The Argives are quite eager
to set sail homeward, leaving Troy behind them.   1050
Do what you have to do, then you can go
back with your sons to where you've settled *my* child.

> *(Exit Polymestor, his sons, Hecuba, and
> the Servant into Agamemnon's tent.)*

CHORUS:xxx
Perhaps it's time for you to come to justice.
Just like a man who falls
into the swirling waters   1055
far from a harbor, you
will be shunted sideways, sprawling,
reft of your heart's desire.
You took a life! You're bound

1060   *to Justice and the gods,*
two debts falling due together:
destruction, destruction awaits you.
You'll find that time belies your expectations;
the road that you chose
1065   *descends straight to Hades.*
The hand that will drag you down
belongs to no warrior.

POLYMESTOR: *(From within; he screams in agony.)*
I'm blinded! Where's the daylight? Aaah, my eyes!

CHORUS:
Listen, friends—the Thracian gentleman's wailing.

POLYMESTOR:
1070   Aaah, my children! Alas, your cruel slaughter!

CHORUS:
My friends, new evils have been done inside.

POLYMESTOR:
You won't escape me, though your feet are swift.
I'll bash this house down, break through every corner!
My hand's my weapon—watch now, as it strikes!

CHORUS:
1075   Shall we fall in to help? The time is ripe;
Hecuba and the women might need allies.

(Enter Hecuba from the tent, closing the entrance
behind her and addressing Polymestor within.)

HECUBA:
Batter away, spare nothing! Bash the doors down!
Your eyes have lost their brightness now—for good!
You'll never see your sons alive: I killed them!

CHORUS:
1080   What? Have you subdued our Thracian guest,
and gained the upper hand, just as you say?

HECUBA:
You'll see him in a moment, staggering
blindly from the house, with a blind and wayward
footstep, and you'll see his two sons' bodies—
I killed them, with these heroic Trojan women.   1085
He's come to justice, paid me what he owed.
Here he comes now. I'll get out of the way
and keep my distance; his Thracian spirit seethes
with rage that's very difficult to withstand.

(Enter Polymestor, blinded and walking on
all fours; he has succeeded in pushing open
the entrance to the tent. The bodies of his
sons are carried out of the tent by women and
placed on the ground. Polymestor sings.)

POLYMESTOR:
Alas, oh alas.   1090
Where can I stand? Can I walk?
Where can I find a haven?
Like a fierce mountain beast
I scramble on my hands
tracking them—where to turn, now: 1095
is it this way, or that?
How can I catch the man-slaying
daughters of Ilion
who have destroyed me?
Accursed girls of Phrygia   1100
who dared dreadful deeds—
oh, where have they flown?
Do they crouch in the corners?

Helios, heal me, heal me!
If only you could restore   1105
the light that was there
beneath my bloodied eyelid!

Quiet now—what was that?
I just heard a footfall
of women trying to hide.   1110
Oh, where shall I pounce
to feed on my prey?

Their bones and their flesh
will be the bestial meal
1115 on which I shall dare
to gorge till I'm full
avenging myself
for this outrage, this insult.

Where, where am I going?

1120 Deserting my slaughtered
sons, so the bacchants
of Hades can take them
and hack up their bodies?
A wild mountain blood-feast
1125 cast out for the dogs!

Where can I stand? Where can I take my rest,
furling my linen sail
like a seagoing ship with its hawsers?
How can I guard my sons
1130 where they lie in this lair of destruction?

CHORUS:
The evils you've endured are hard to bear;
shameful deeds claim terrible repayments.[xxxi]

POLYMESTOR: *(Singing.)*
Aah! Hear me, spear-bearing host
of Thrace, land of horses—
1135 men in arms, race devoted to Ares!
Oh hear me, Achaeans!
Sons of Atreus, hear me!
I cry aloud, I cry for help:
come here, approach, by the gods!
1140 Does anyone hear me? Will no one come? Why the delay?
Women destroyed me,
captive women!
What I've suffered is terrible, terrible!
Alas for this outrage.
1145 Where can I turn? Where can I go?
Shall I fly up to the heavens, the palace aloft in the sky,
where blazing rays of fire shoot from the eyes of Orion

and Sirius? Or shall I flit, poor me,
down to the glossy black skin of the waters encircling Hades?

CHORUS:
It's understandable, when one has suffered   1150
unbearable sorrow, to exit this sad life.

(Enter Agamemnon from the camp, with attendants.)

AGAMEMNON:
I heard a shout—a racket—so I came here.
Echo, the daughter of the mountain crag,[43]
launched a troubled wail across the camp.
If we didn't know the Greek spear had already   1155
brought down the Phrygian towers, then that sound
would have frightened us tremendously, I tell you.

POLYMESTOR:
Most welcome, most beloved Agamemnon!
I recognized your voice. See how I suffer!

AGAMEMNON:
Ah, Polymestor! Poor man, who destroyed you?   1160
Who blinded you, and caused this blood to stream
down from your eyes? Who killed these children? Truly,
whoever he was, he must have hated you.

POLYMESTOR:
Hecuba and the captive women destroyed me.
No—what they did was much worse than destruction!   1165

AGAMEMNON:
Hecuba, did you really dare this dreadful
deed, and leave him helpless, as he says?

POLYMESTOR:
Oh god, what's that? Is *she* somewhere nearby?

---

43. We do not know whether Echo had any mythology at this period; here
she is the "daughter of the mountain crag" because echoes are heard in
mountain valleys.

Tell me where she is: I'll rip her apart
1170 with my bare hands; her skin will stream with blood.

AGAMEMNON:
What's wrong with you?

POLYMESTOR:
                        I beg you, by the gods,
let me get my hands on her! I'm going insane!

AGAMEMNON:
Restrain yourself. Cast the barbarity
out of your heart, and speak, so I can listen
1175 to each of you in turn, and, in accordance
with justice, judge the reason why you suffer.

POLYMESTOR:
Yes, I will speak.
                        There was a son of Priam
and Hecuba, the youngest, Polydorus.
His father Priam sent him out of Troy—
1180 suspecting that the city would be taken—
and gave him to me, to raise in my own home.
I killed him. Listen, now, and hear the reason;
I acted wisely, and with forethought, fearing
that if the child survived he'd be your foe:
1185 he'd rally and reunify the Trojans.
Then, when the Achaeans realized a son
of Priam was still living, they'd return,
bring their army back to Phrygia,
and take the Thracian plain for spoils and plunder;
1190 Troy's neighbors would again go through the evils
by which we've been so recently undone.

My lord, when Hecuba learned her child's fate
she drew me in by promising to tell
where Priam's sons had hidden certain coffers,
1195 coffers of gold, in Ilion. She drew me
inside her home, alone, with just my sons,
so no one else would learn this information.
I sat down on a couch and took my rest.

The girls of Troy were inside—lots of them,
to my left hand and my right. They took their seats	1200
beside me, as if I were an old friend;
they held my robes up to the light to see
the Edonian handiwork, and praised the weaving.[44]
Some others saw the Thracian pikes I held
and stripped me of them both. Those who were mothers	1205
were smitten with my boys; they tossed them up
playfully in their hands, and then maneuvered
the boys away from me by passing them
from hand to hand. Their gentle conversation
was peaceful as a windless sea, and then	1210
suddenly—it was unbelievable—
from somewhere in their robes they pull out daggers
and stab my children! Other women (now
no longer friends, but wartime foes)[xxxii] take hold
of my hands; they pin my arms and legs. I try	1215
to help my boys, but if I raise my head
they yank my hair, and if I try to move
my hands, the mob of women holds me back.
I get nowhere—poor me. Last of all,
—pain worse than pain!—they pull their brooches out	1220
and—dreadful deed!—they stab me in the eyes;[45]
my pupils[xxxiii] stream with blood.
                              They scattered, fled
throughout the shelter. Like a beast, I sprang
after those murderous dogs, and I sniffed out
every corner, like a hunter, bashing	1225
and battering.
              This is what I've had to suffer
all for the sake of doing you a favor,
Agamemnon, by killing your wartime foe.

I'll tell you something else, and I'll be brief.
If any man before has told the tale	1230
of women's wickedness, or tells it now

---

44. Edonian = Thracian; the region was famous for its textiles.
45. They blind him with the pins from their dresses, just as Oedipus in
Sophocles' *Oedipus Tyrannus* uses Jocasta's to blind himself.

or ever plans to, here's the gist of it:
no race like them is bred on sea or land,
as everyone who deals with them discovers.

CHORUS:

1235   Don't be brash, and don't blame your own troubles
on the female race, or lump us all together.^{xxxiv}

HECUBA:

Agamemnon, a person's tongue should never
surpass his deeds. If he acts decently,
then let his words be decent. If he's malicious,
1240   his words, too, should be flawed, and he should never
be able to speak well for unjust causes.
Yes, some can—they've mastered every detail
of this technique. They're clever, but in the end
they can't sustain it; they're totally destroyed.
1245   It happens every time. There, Agamemnon,
you have my prelude; now I'll turn to him.

You say you killed my son to spare the Achaeans
a second struggle, and to please Agamemnon.
You are the worst! Barbarians, for one thing,
1250   would not be friendly to the Greeks, and could not.
What "favor" were you doing? What gratitude
were you so eager for? Perhaps you hoped
to gain an in-law? Or were you already
a blood relation? Well, what *was* your reason?
1255   To stop the Greeks from sailing here again
and cutting down your seedlings? Who'd believe that?
It was the gold (if you by any chance
would like to tell the truth!) that killed my son,
and your own hope for profit. Tell me this:
1260   when Troy held sway, protected by her ramparts,
and Priam lived, and Hector's spear still flourished,
if what you wanted was the gratitude
of this man here, and you were nurturing
my child in your home, why didn't you just kill him
1265   *then,* or hand him over to the Argives?
Instead, once we had faded from the daylight
and smoke rose from our ruined town, disclosing

that we were captive now, owned by our foes,
then you killed the guest-friend at your hearth!

There's more; just listen. It does not reflect   1270
well on you. If you were really friendly
with those Achaeans, then you should have given
the gold to them—as you admit, it wasn't
yours to keep, but his—

    (Gesturing to the body of Polydorus.)

                they needed money
and they had been here, strangers far from home,   1275
for a long time.[46] But even now you won't
release it from your hand; it's in your house.
Look: if you had only raised my child
the way you should have, nurtured him and kept him
safe, you'd have a handsome reputation.   1280
Good friends stand out most clearly in hard times;
when things are easy, friends are everywhere.
If you had needed money, and my son
enjoyed good fortune, then he would have been
your ample treasury! But as it is,   1285
it's over: you don't have him as a friend,
you don't have any profit from the gold,
your sons are gone, and you are in this state.

Agamemnon, if you help this man,
you won't look good; you'll benefit a host   1290
who's impious, untrustworthy, unholy,
unjust. We'll say that wicked men delight you
because you yourself are wicked. Though of course
I wouldn't want to chastise you, my lord.

CHORUS:
    Ah! Decent facts are always a fine basis   1295
    for making one's case decently in words.

---

46. The Homeric poems take place before the invention of money, so this
is an anachronism. But everyone in the Greek world would understand a
military expedition's need for cash.

AGAMEMNON:
I find it burdensome to be the judge
in someone else's plight, but I'm compelled.
It would be disgraceful, since I've taken
1300   this matter in hand, to push it back away.
Here's how it seems to me: you killed your guest-friend
not to win my gratitude, nor as a favor
to the Achaeans. You wanted to have that gold,
to keep it in your home, and now you're saying
1305   whatever you think will get you out of trouble.
Perhaps it doesn't mean much to you people
to kill a guest. We Greeks find it appalling.
How, then, if I decreed you'd acted justly,
would I avoid blame? No, I couldn't. Since
1310   you had the nerve to do something so loathsome,
prepare to suffer something most unwelcome.

POLYMESTOR:
Defeated by a woman—a slave! I'm brought
to justice by those worse than me, it seems.

HECUBA:
Justice, yes. Are you not in the wrong?

POLYMESTOR:
1315   Alas, my sons. Alas, my eyes. Poor me.

HECUBA:
What, does it hurt? Do you think *I* don't grieve?

POLYMESTOR:
You delight in this atrocity, you fiend . . .

HECUBA:
Shouldn't I delight in taking vengeance?

POLYMESTOR:
. . . but not for long. The waters of the sea . . .

HECUBA:
1320   Will carry me to Greece? Imagine that!

POLYMESTOR:
. . . will cover you, when you fall from the masthead.

HECUBA:
By whom will I be forced to make this leap?

POLYMESTOR:
You'll scamper up the ship's mast on your own.

HECUBA:
How will I do it? Will my back sprout wings?

POLYMESTOR:
You will become a dog with blazing eyes.[47]

1325

HECUBA:
How do you know that I will change my shape?

POLYMESTOR:
From Dionysus, prophet to the Thracians.[48]

HECUBA:
And yet he didn't warn you of your troubles?

POLYMESTOR:
No. If he had, you never would have tricked me.

HECUBA:
Will I die here, or live? What is my fate?[xxxv]

1330

POLYMESTOR:
You will die. Your tomb will bear the name . . .

---

47. This is the oldest attestation of Hecuba's metamorphosis into a dog, but Euripides is unlikely to have invented it. Greeks associated dogs with both shamelessness and tenacious loyalty; it is unclear exactly what it connotes here.

48. Greeks frequently associate Dionysus with Thrace, and Herodotus says that the Thracians worship only Ares, Artemis, and Dionysus (5.7). He also mentions a mountain oracle of Dionysus in Thrace (7.111.2). Euripides often displays such ethnographic knowledge.

HECUBA:
What? Some name that chimes with my new shape?

POLYMESTOR:
"Poor Bitch's Grave," marking the way for sailors.[49]

HECUBA:
I don't even care, now that you've come to justice.

POLYMESTOR:
1335   Cassandra, too, will die. Her fate compels it.

HECUBA:
I spit on your predictions. Tell your *own* fate!

POLYMESTOR: *(Indicating Agamemnon.)*
His wife—a lethal homemaker!—will kill her.

HECUBA:
Keep madness far off from Tyndareos' child!

POLYMESTOR:
She'll swing an axe on high and kill *him,* too.[50]

AGAMEMNON:
1340   What are you, mad? Are you in love with trouble?

POLYMESTOR:
Go on and kill me! In Argos, you'll bathe in blood.

AGAMEMNON:
Servants, drag him away from here by force.

POLYMESTOR:
Does it hurt to hear this?

---

49. Cynossema, "dog's monument," is a promontory in the Hellespont (Dardanelles) near modern Kilitbahir.

50. Agamemnon and Cassandra were murdered by Agamemnon's wife, Clytemnestra (daughter of Tyndareos and sister of Helen).

AGAMEMNON: *(To his attendants.)*
                            Won't you shut him up?

POLYMESTOR:
  Go ahead—I've spoken.

AGAMEMNON:
                            Take him this instant
  and cast him out on some deserted island;   1345
  his mouth is far too brash.[51]

        *(Attendants drag Polymestor off in
        the direction of the camp.)*

                            You, Hecuba,
  poor woman, come and bury these two corpses.
  Daughters of Troy, you must go to the tents
  of your masters now, for I can see already:
  the winds have picked up that will send us homeward.   1350
  May we have good sailing to our fatherland
  and may we see that all is well at home
  once we've found deliverance from these struggles.

        *(Exit Hecuba, Agamemnon, and remaining attendants,
        carrying the body of Polydorus, toward the camp.)*[xxxvi]

CHORUS:
  Let us go to the tents, friends; let's go to the harbor;
  it's time to take up the toils of our masters.   1355
  Compulsion is brutal.

        (Exit the Chorus, following the others.)

---

51. An ironic reframing of *Odyssey* 3.270–72, where Nestor tells
Telemachus how Aegisthus had the singer whom Agamemnon had
appointed as Clytemnestra's guardian abandoned on a desert island.

Trojan Women

Trojan Women: Cast of Characters

POSEIDON	god of the sea; brother of Zeus
ATHENA	daughter of Zeus; also called Pallas
HECUBA	queen of Troy
CHORUS	women of Troy, now captives of the Greek army
TALTHYBIUS	Greek herald
CASSANDRA	daughter of Hecuba
ANDROMACHE	widow of Hecuba's son Hector
MENELAUS	brother of Agamemnon; co-leader of Greek attack on Troy
HELEN	wife of Menelaus

Trojan Women

SCENE: *The Greek camp outside the city of Troy, which*
the Greek army has devastated and burned.
Hecuba is lying on the ground in front of the
stage building, which represents the tent of
Agamemnon where the captive women are
housed. One side entrance leads to the rest of the
Greek camp and the ships, the other to the city
of Troy.

(*Enter Poseidon.*)

POSEIDON:
I've left the salty depths of the Aegean
where Nereids dance, their lovely footfalls swirling
in choruses below the waves. I am
Poseidon. These stone towers, true and plumb,
that gird this Trojan land, I built myself   5
along with Phoebus.[1] Since then, I have always
felt kindly toward the city of the Phrygians—

which now lies ruined, smoldering, destroyed
by Argive spears.[2] Athena's strategies
inspired Epeius, a Phocian from Parnassus,[3]   10
to build a horse—pregnant with armed men,

---

1. In Homer's *Iliad*, Poseidon is hostile to Troy, because King Laomedon refused to pay him for building Troy's walls and threatened him. He does not understand why Apollo (who Poseidon once says helped build the walls, though he elsewhere says that Apollo tended Laomedon's flocks: *Iliad* 7.452–3, 21.441–57) favors the Trojans. Making Poseidon pro-Trojan may be a Euripidean innovation, allowing the play to begin with a reconciliation of previously opposed gods.

2. Tragedy freely uses the various epic terms for the Greeks at Troy: "Argive" here, "Achaean" at 17, "Danaans" at 739.

3. Mount Parnassus is in western Phocis. Euripides likes such geographical precision, although it does not really matter where Epeius came from.

117

a ruinous idol—and send it through the gates.[i]
The gods' groves are deserted, and their shrines
stream with gore. Beside the altar base
15   of Zeus who Guards the Hearth, Priam fell dead.

Great quantities of gold are being sent
to the Achaean ships, along with Phrygian spoils.
The Greeks who came here to assault this town
are waiting for a wind to send them back
20   to wives and children, a happy sight; they've been here
through ten long growing seasons.
                                        As for me,
I've been defeated by the gods who took
the Phrygians down together, Argive Hera[4]
and Athena. I am leaving glorious Ilion,
25   leaving my altars. A town that's been deserted
tends to neglect its gods, stint on their honors.

Scamander[5] echoes with the panicked moans
of captive women, matched by lottery
with their new masters. Some of them will go
30   to Arcadia, some to Thessaly, some to Athens,
to Theseus' sons, the chiefs.[6] The rest, the girls
picked out especially for the commanders,
are in this dwelling. With them is the Spartan,
Helen. She's a captive—rightly so.

35   Look at this wretched woman lying down
at the entrance to the tent. That's Hecuba.
She's weeping; she has many things to weep for.
Her daughter, poor Polyxena, has died

---

4. Although at 9 "Argive" means no more than "Greek," as an epithet of
Hera it refers to the city of Argos, of which she was the tutelary goddess.

5. Scamander is the main river of the Trojan plain.

6. Arcadia is not important in Homer; Euripides probably includes it here
partly because it had been politically important recently—an army of
Athenians, Argives, and the Arcadian city of Mantinea had been defeated
by Sparta in 418 BCE near Mantinea—and partly to locate Athens at the
center of the Greek world, balanced by Thessaly in the north and Arcadia
in the south. As usual, Euripides makes Athens more prominent than the
epic tradition did.

at Achilles' monument, but Hecuba
doesn't know that yet.[7] Priam is gone,   40
their sons are gone. The girl whom Lord Apollo
left with her virginity—Cassandra,[8]
the wild one—will be taken to the bed
of Agamemnon, violently, without
regard for piety or for the god,   45
in a shadow marriage.
                        Farewell, once-fortunate city;
smooth stone towers, farewell. If Zeus's daughter
had not destroyed you, you would still be standing.

    (Enter Athena.)

ATHENA:
My father's brother, honored and revered
among the gods, I'd like to set aside   50
our former animosity, and speak.

POSEIDON:
You may do so. Kinship, Lady Athena,
is like a magic charm. Please, speak your mind.

ATHENA:
Thanks; you're very kind. I'd like to broach
a topic that concerns us both, my lord.   55

POSEIDON:
Do you have some announcement or some news
from Zeus, perhaps, or from some other god?

---

7. Hecuba does not find out exactly what happened to Polyxena until
644–45. The phrase "but Hecuba / doesn't know that yet" translates the
single Greek word "secretly," and while the main point is that Hecuba
does not know, the word implies a very different sequence of events from
those in *Hecuba*, where Polyxena's sacrifice follows an open debate in the
assembly and is a large public spectacle.

8. Poseidon implies that Apollo chose to leave Cassandra a virgin. In the
usual story, he granted her prophecy in return for her sexual compliance,
and when she reneged he punished her with never having her prophecies
believed. That does not seem to be the story here.

ATHENA:
> No, not that—it has to do with Troy,
> the ground on which we walk. Can we join forces?

POSEIDON:
60
> Why? Have you dropped your animosity
> and now you pity this scorched, ruined town?

ATHENA:
> First, tell me: will you speak with me, and join me
> in wanting what I want? I have a plan.

POSEIDON:
> Of course. But I must know: what *do* you want?
65
> Are you here for the Greeks, or for the Phrygians?

ATHENA:
> The Trojans were my enemies, but now
> I'm on their side. I want to hurt the Greeks.

POSEIDON:
> Why do you jump around like that? Your whims
> drive you to hate, and love, excessively.

ATHENA:
70
> You do know of their outrage in my temple?

POSEIDON:
> Yes; Ajax took Cassandra violently.[9]

ATHENA:
> The Greeks stood by and didn't say a word.

POSEIDON:
> And yet they ravaged Troy with help from you.

---

9. The Ajax who assaulted Cassandra in Athena's temple is Ajax son of
Oïleus, from Locris. The gods killed him on his way home from Troy.

ATHENA:
That's why I want to harm them—with *your* help.

POSEIDON:
I'm at your service. Tell me what you'll do.   75

ATHENA:
I'll make their voyage home a bitter passage.[10]

POSEIDON:
On dry land, or upon the salt sea waves?

ATHENA:
When they are sailing home from Ilion.
Zeus will send down rain and endless hail,
disturb the sky with dark gusts. He will give me   80
his fiery bolt to strike the Argive ships,
igniting them with flame. Your part will be
to make the Aegean roar with surging waves
and gurging eddies, filling up the cove
with corpses when the fleet comes near Euboea.[11]   85
That will teach the Achaeans to revere
my shrines, and all the other gods, from now on.

POSEIDON:
So be it. There's no need for lengthy speeches;
I'll do this favor, agitate the waves
of the briny Aegean Sea. The jagged coasts   90
of Mykonos and Delos, Scyros, Lemnos,

---

10. This plan is unique in tragedy, since a divine prologue normally
foretells what will happen during the play, not after it ends. A prophetic
individual (like Polymestor in *Hecuba*) or a final divine epiphany often
predicts its aftermath.

11. The long, narrow island of Euboea, which runs along the east coast of
Boeotia, was the home of Nauplius. *Palamedes*, the second play Euripides
presented before *Trojan Women* in the original production, showed the
judicial murder of Nauplius' son Palamedes, and traditionally Nauplius
took revenge by setting false beacons that lured the homecoming Greeks
onto the rocks during the storm Poseidon and Athena are planning here.

and Caphareus' cape[12] will be awash
in corpses.
              Go to Olympus now, and take
the fiery shafts from your father's hands. Keep watch
95   for when the Argive fleet lets out the reefs.

That man's an idiot who ravages
cities, and consigns their holy temples
and tombs—the sacred places of the dead—
to stark desertion. He will die himself.

        (*Exit Poseidon and Athena. Hecuba rises
        slowly as she begins to chant her lament.*)

HECUBA:
100   Raise your head from the ground, lift your neck from the dirt;
       rise now, consider your fate! It is bleak.
       This is no longer Troy; we're no longer in charge.
       This fate has descended upon you; endure it.
       Sail with the changes, sail with the current,
105   sail *with* your fate, not against it. Don't turn
       your prow toward the oncoming wave; it will crush you.
       Aah!
       I have reason to groan. All I had is now gone.
       My country has vanished, my children, my husband.

       Our importance, our ancestry—as it turns out
110   they meant nothing at all. Those sails have been shortened.

       Why remain silent? Why bother speaking?
       Why spend my breath on a useless lament?

       Unhappy me for the fate that's descended
       heavy upon me, forcing me down
115   to sprawl on my back. This is brutal—my head,
       and my ribs!—how I wish I could roll from one side

---

12. The islands listed cover a wide area of the Aegean: Lemnos in the
northeast is relatively close to Troy, Scyros further south and west, while
Mykonos and Delos are in the center of the Cyclades. Cape Caphareus
is a rocky promontory in southern Euboea, the site of Nauplius' false
beacons.

to the other, from starboard to port, shift my spine,
swirl through the swells of my tears and my keening.

This is the Muse that moves the forlorn
to tell of their ruin—a tune with no dancing.   120

     (Hecuba sings.)[ii]

Prows that were aimed
toward Ilion, our
sacred city, swift oars
that swept through the violet-tinged
sea, through the gentle   125
harbors of Hellas
(to the tune of the hateful
paean that flowed
from the flute and the gentle
voice of the syrinx):[13]   130

when you came to the bay
of Troy you let down
your woven Egyptian
cables;[14] you came for
Menelaus's wife,   135
the hateful one! She's
a disgrace and an outrage
to Castor,[15] to Sparta;[iii]
she is the slayer
of Priam, who sired   140
fifty children! And she is the one who has driven
Hecuba—poor me!—onto these shoals.
I am ruined; I'm shattered.

---

13. The paean was performed on various occasions, including before battle, but it was usually sung. This paean seems to be an instrumental piece.

14. The cables are Egyptian because they are made of papyrus from Egypt.

15. Castor and Polydeuces (or Pollux), the Dioscuri (sons of Zeus), are Helen's brothers.

Alas for my station, this place I must take
145   by the tent of Agamemnon.

A sorrowful slave—
an old woman whose head
has been pitifully ravaged—
I'm dragged from my home.

150   Poor wives of the Trojans
whose weapons once flashed
with the brightness of bronze!
Poor brides, with your woeful
weddings! Now Ilion
155   smolders—so hopeless
our moans! I'll begin
our cacophonous chorus,
set it in motion, just like a bird
leading her chicks, but our song is so changed:

160   nothing at all like it used to be once
with Priam still holding the scepter;
I'd lead the dancing, the footfalls all striking
in rhythm to honor the Phrygian gods.[16]

*(Enter the first half-chorus of Trojan
women from the tent, singing.)*

FIRST HALF-CHORUS:

[Strophe 1]

Hecuba, what are you saying? I heard your cry
165   from inside, and I'd like to know, what does it mean,
this pitiful plaint? Fear darts through the breasts
of the women of Troy who are gathered inside
bewailing our slavery, here in this tent.

HECUBA:
The Achaeans, my dears, are heading for their ships
170   already; their hands are reaching for the oars.

---

16. Phrygia was an ancient state of west-central Anatolia, in Euripides'
time part of the Persian Empire. In tragedy Troy was often assimilated to
Phrygia.

FIRST HALF-CHORUS:
Is it already time to be led to the ship,
leave my country behind? What is it they want?

HECUBA:
It looks like our ruin. I don't know.

FIRST HALF-CHORUS:
Oh no, oh no!

> *(Turning back to the tent door to
> address those still inside.)*

Poor daughters of Troy, come out of your house   175
to hear of your heartache;
the Argives are preparing to go home.

HECUBA:
Oh sorrow, sorrow.
Don't send Cassandra out here,
the maenad, the bacchante,[17]   180
to be shamed by the Argives, to pain me,
to hurt me still more.
Oh no, oh no.
Unhappy Troy, you have vanished.
Unhappy are those who are forced to leave you: 185
those who are living, and those who've been crushed.

> *(Enter the second half-chorus from the tent, singing.)*

SECOND HALF-CHORUS:

[Antistrophe 1]

Trembling, I've left Agamemnon's tent to hear
what you're saying, my queen. Are the Argives, alas,
intending to kill me? Or are they on board
their vessels already, preparing to go,   190
to push through the waves with the oars at the sterns?

---

17. Maenads and bacchantes are women engaged in ecstatic worship of
Dionysus; Euripides uses Dionysiac language freely for abnormal mental
states, even when Dionysus is not the god involved.

HECUBA:
I have come here, my dear, in terror—shaking hard,
awake since the dawn; my soul's been stunned with fear.

SECOND HALF-CHORUS:
Has a messenger already come from the Greeks?
195   Tell me, where will I sleep? Whose slave will I be?

HECUBA:
The lottery will be soon, I suppose.

SECOND HALF-CHORUS:
Oh no, oh no!
Poor unhappy me, where will I be led:
to Argos, to Phthia,[18]
200   or to an island, far away from Troy?

HECUBA:
Oh torment, torment.
Where will I serve as a slave,
a white-haired crone, a drone?
I look just like a corpse, I'm the image
205   of the dearly departed.
Ah me, ah me.
Maybe I'll stand in a doorway,
a withered old sentry, a babysitter—
I who was honored as sovereign of Troy!

CHORUS: *(The two half-choruses sing together.)*

[Strophe 2]

210   What piteous cries could you find
to bewail this insult? Never again will Mount Ida[19]
be called my home as I weave at the loom.

---

18. Argos in tragedy is often named in place of nearby Mycenae, Agamemnon's home (a very minor place in classical times); Phthia, in northern Greece, was Achilles' home.
19. Mount Ida lies to the southeast of Troy and is often associated with the city.

I'm taking my very last look at my parent's house,[iv]
my very last look. More heartache awaits:
I'll be brought to the bed of a Greek   215
(may that night and that fate both vanish!)
or, at Peirene,[20] a pitiful servant, be sent
with my pitcher to fill at the streams of the sacred spring.
I hope I will go to the glorious land
of Theseus, blessed by fortune.   220
Keep me away, I pray,
from Helen's hated home beside the eddies
of the Eurotas, where, as a slave, I would meet
Menelaus, the ravager of Troy.

[Antistrophe 2]

I've heard that the sacred terrain   225
by Peneus River, beautiful base of Olympus,
is fruitful, prosperous, plenteous, rich.
That place would be my second choice if I cannot go
to Theseus' land, that hallowed terrain.
And I hear that Hephaestus's isle   230
facing Carthage, the land of Aetna—
Sicily, mother of mountains—is often announced
as the homeland of those who are crowned for their excellence,
and so is the country right next to the blue
Ionian Sea, which Crathis   235
nurtures with hallowed streams
that tinge the hair with flecks of golden fire:
beautiful torrent that blesses a land well known
for the outstanding men who call it home.[21]

Look: a messenger's coming this way from the Greeks,   240
a steward of news from the army, his footfalls

---

20. Pirene was a famous spring at Corinth. Sparta was on the Eurotas.
In this passage, the Chorus prefer Athens and its allies to Sparta and its
allies.

21. In lines 225–39 the Chorus praise Thessaly, with the Peneus River
and Mount Olympus; Sicily; and Thurii in southern Italy, where the
Crathis River was believed to dye hair. These were probably all places
where Euripides had admirers, and he may have been flattering prospec-
tive audiences.

hitting the ground with great speed.
What report will he bring? What's the word? We must listen;
we're already slaves of the Dorian land.[22]

(Enter Talthybius. In the following passage
Talthybius speaks and Hecuba sings.)

TALTHYBIUS:
245   Hecuba—you see, I know your name;
in times past, I brought messages quite often
to Troy from the Achaean army. I'm
Talthybius—you know me—and I'm here
with news to report.

HECUBA:
               Oh my friends, dear women,
250   *this is what I've feared for a long time now!*

TALTHYBIUS:
The lots have now been drawn. Was that your fear?

HECUBA:
Aah! Will it be a city in Phthia,
in Thessaly? Or in the land of Cadmus?[23]

TALTHYBIUS:
You're not all together; each allotment's separate.

HECUBA:
255   *Who received whom? Which woman of Troy*
will be fortunate in her fate?

TALTHYBIUS:
I know; I'll tell you. Listen: one at a time!

---

22. The Dorians were one of the three major divisions among the Greeks;
Sparta was Dorian (the others were Ionian, which included Athens, and
Aeolian).

23. Thebes is the land of Cadmus, who settled there after traveling from
Phoenicia.

HECUBA:
Tell me, who received my daughter, unhappy Cassandra?

TALTHYBIUS:
Agamemnon picked her out especially.

HECUBA:
Oh, no—as a slave for his Spartan wife?[24]   260

TALTHYBIUS:
No, for his bed: a kind of shadow marriage.

HECUBA:
But she was Phoebus's virgin, and that was her prize of honor:
an unbedded life was granted to her by the golden-haired
god![25]

TALTHYBIUS:
The arrows of Desire struck Agamemnon.

HECUBA:
O my child, fling down your hallowed boughs   265
and the sacred garlands you wear!

TALTHYBIUS:
Yes—a royal bed is quite an honor.

HECUBA:
What about the child you took from me most recently?
Where is she?

TALTHYBIUS:
Polyxena, you mean? Or someone else?   270

---

24. Agamemnon's wife, Clytemnestra, was Helen's sister. When
Agamemnon and Cassandra returned home, she murdered them both.

25. Hecuba states more explicitly what Poseidon implied in the prologue,
that Apollo granted Cassandra virginity. Agamemnon's sexual use of her
thereby approaches sacrilege.

HECUBA:
Polyxena. To whom was she yoked by the drawing of lots?

TALTHYBIUS:
She has been stationed at Achilles' tomb.

HECUBA:
Alas, alas. The child I bore—a grave attendant.
Tell me, my friend, what law
275　*of the Greeks decreed this, what custom?*

TALTHYBIUS:
Count your child blessed. All is well with her.

HECUBA:
What do you mean?
Does she live, can she still see the sun?

TALTHYBIUS:
Her fate releases her from all her struggles.

HECUBA:
280　*And the wife of Hector, skilled fighter in bronze,*
poor Andromache—what is her fortune?

TALTHYBIUS:
Achilles' son picked her to be his prize.

HECUBA:
And what about me? Whose servant will I be,
an old woman who hobbles three-leggèd, a staff in my hand?

TALTHYBIUS:
285　Odysseus, lord of Ithaca, drew your lot.

HECUBA:
Oh sorrow, sorrow.
Batter my shorn head, drag
my nails across my cheeks!
Oh no, ah me.
290　*I've been assigned as a slave to a loathsome*

foe of justice, a wild beast, deceptive
and lawless, who twists with his double-edged tongue
everything this way and that; what was loved
becomes hated when he's had his way with it![26]
Weep for me, daughters of Troy.   295
It's over: my fate has been sealed;
my lot has been drawn, the unluckiest one.

CHORUS:
You know your fortune, mistress. What of mine?
What Hellene, what Achaean will possess me?

TALTHYBIUS:
You servants: go now, bring Cassandra here   300
as quickly as you can, so I can put her
in the general's hands. After that I'll bring
the other captive women to their masters,
according to the lottery.

> (Some of the women begin to open the door of
> the tent, revealing a glimpse of fire within.)

What's that?
That flash of blazing pine—what's going on?   305
Are the Trojan women burning down their quarters,
or what? Are they attempting to set fire
to their own bodies? Do they want to die
since they're about to be shipped off to Argos?
This kind of grief, for someone used to freedom,   310
certainly chafes hard against the neck.

Hey, open up! This may be what *they* want,
but the Greeks would hate it, and *I* might get the blame.

> (Enter Cassandra from the tent, brandishing torches.)

---

26. The wily Odysseus of epic often becomes, in tragedy, the essence of
what people feared in contemporary rhetorical teaching—that it produced
politicians who could and would use any clever argument for their own
purposes.

HECUBA:
There is no fire.
It's my child, Cassandra
315   the maenad; here she comes—she's moving fast!

CASSANDRA:

[Strophe]

Raise the flame, bring it here! I honor this temple—
come look, come look!—
with the blaze of torchlight. O lord Hymenaeus![27]
Blessed is the bridegroom,
320   and I too am blessed: I'll be taken to Argos
to be married, recline in a royal bed!
Hymen, lord Hymenaeus!
Since you, O mother, persist in grieving
for my dead father—weeping and groaning—
325   and the homeland we loved,
I raise the wedding torch myself[28]—
this glowing flame, this gleam of light—
making it shine out for you, lord Hymenaeus
and for you, O Hecate;[29]
330   just as we always do
for a maiden's wedding night!

[Antistrophe]

Toss your foot in the air, come dance, lead the chorus!
Eu'an, eu'oi![30]
Come and dance, just as in the days of my father's

---

27. Hymenaeus or Hymen is the god of the wedding ceremony, as well as the song for the torchlight procession to the groom's house that was central to wedding ritual.

28. The bride's mother normally held torches for the procession.

29. Hecate is surprising here. She sometimes overlaps with Artemis, who was important at weddings because she was the protector of unmarried girls, but more often Hecate is the goddess of witchcraft. Cassandra's invocation hints at the sinister nature of this "marriage."

30. These cries are characteristic of the ecstasy of possession by Dionysus.

most blessèd fortune! 335
The chorus is holy; come lead it, O Phoebus.
Decked in laurels, I sacrifice at your shrine.
Hymen, O Hymenaeus!
Come dance, O mother; come lead the chorus,
come let your footsteps swirl in a circle, 340
in the steps we love most!
Come shout aloud the wedding-hymn,
sing out your blessings for the bride!
Phrygian girls in your lovely robes, come out now,
sing and dance for my husband; 345
sing for my marriage bed
and the fate I'll soon embrace!

CHORUS:
My queen, you'd better stop your bacchic daughter
before she dances into the Greek camp.

HECUBA:
Hephaestus, wedding torchbearer, this flame 350
you kindle now is painful, desolate.[31]
It's not what we had hoped for. O my child,
I never thought your wedding would be held
at Argive spearpoint, never saw you as
a captive. Give me those.

(Hecuba takes the torches from Cassandra
and extinguishes them on the ground.)

                    Running out 355
like a maenad, waving fire around—my child,
it isn't right. Your sense of wise restraint
has not returned. Your mind is still affected.

(Hecuba hands the extinguished torches to the women.)

Take these torches inside now, daughters of Troy,
and let your tears replace her wedding songs. 360

---

31. Hephaestus is the god of fire.

CASSANDRA:
 I am victorious, mother! Crown my head
 with garlands, celebrate my royal marriage.
 Escort me! And if I seem less than eager,
 drive me on by force. If Loxias[32]
365 is real, then glorious Agamemnon, lord
 of the Achaeans, when he takes me as his bride
 will enter a marriage more troublesome than Helen's,
 for I will kill him.[33] I'll exact the blood-price
 he owes me for my brothers and my father;
370 I'll ravage *his* home as he ravaged mine.

 But never mind these details. I won't sing
 of the axe that's going to bite into my neck—
 and others' necks, too—or the mother-slaying
 strife that's set in motion by my marriage,
375 or the wreckage of the house of Atreus.[34]
 Instead, I'll show you how our city, Troy,
 enjoys more blessings than the Greeks. You'll say
 the god possesses me; that's true, but still
 I can step outside my bacchic raving.

380 The Greeks, to hunt down Helen—just one woman,
 just one Cypris—slaughtered tens of thousands.[35]
 Their general, great wise man that he is,
 destroyed what is most precious for what's most
 despicable. He forfeited the joy
385 of children in his home—all for his brother
 and a woman who was willingly abducted!
 Their borders weren't attacked; the lofty towers
 within their fatherland were never taken.
 And yet they perished, man by man, beside

---

32. Loxias is a name of Apollo.

33. Agamemnon's wife Clytemnestra killed him. Although Clytemnestra had several reasons, Cassandra focuses on her resentment that Agamemnon brought Cassandra home as a concubine.

34. Cassandra can refer allusively to Orestes' killing of his mother in revenge for his father Agamemnon, since the story was familiar to everyone.

35. Cypris is Aphrodite, here meaning "object of desire."

Scamander's banks. The war god claimed his victims: 390
they didn't see their children, and their wives
could never wrap them in their burial robes;
they lie in foreign soil, while at home
widows died alone, and parents lost
the children they had raised in vain. No one   395
was there to offer blood-gifts at their graves.[v]

The Trojans, on the other hand, have won
the greatest glory; man by man, they perished
fighting for their country. Yes, the spear
claimed many victims, but all were carried back   400
to their homes by loved ones, wrapped for burial
by kindred hands, and covered up with earth
in their own fatherland. The Phrygians
who didn't die in battle spent their days
with wives and children, cherishing the joy   405
denied to the Achaeans. As for Hector,
what happened to him may seem grim to you,
but listen: he was the best, and he died famous—
thanks to the Achaeans. If they'd stayed home
then Hector's prowess would have been unknown.   410
If Paris hadn't married Zeus's daughter,[36]
his marriage-bond would never have been mentioned.

Yes, anyone with sense steers clear of war.
But if war comes, a fine death is a crown
upon the city's brow; the only shame   415
in dying is to die disgracefully.
So, Mother, there is no need to feel pity
for our land, or for the bedroom that awaits me.
You see, with this marriage I will rip to shreds
the ones that we find most despicable.   420

CHORUS:
You laugh so sweetly at your own misfortunes;
your song and dance may not be on sure footing.

---

36. Helen was the daughter of Zeus and either Leda, wife of Tyndareos,
or the goddess Nemesis ("Retribution").

TALTHYBIUS:
  You'd have to pay for talk like that, young lady—
  what a send-off for the generals!—
425 if Apollo hadn't robbed you of your wits.

  The ones considered wise, as it turns out,
  the high and mighty, really are no better
  than nobodies. The scion of Atreus,[37]
  for example—greatest lord of all the Greeks—
430 succumbed completely to desire for this . . .
  maenad girl he picked out specially.
  Poor simple man that I am, I wouldn't want her—
  at least, not in my bed.
                          As for your praise
  of the Phrygians, and reproaches of the Argives,
435 you're not in your right mind, so I dismiss them:
  the wind can sweep away your words. Come on,
  follow me to the ships. The general
  awaits his lovely bride.

    (To Hecuba.)

                          And you, whenever
  Laertes' son shows up for you, go with him.
440 You'll be his wife's servant; her wise restraint's well known
  among the troops who came to Ilion.[38]

CASSANDRA:
  Oh, what a clever servant! This class of men[39]
  is universally detested; tell me,
  how did they earn the title "messenger,"
445 these errand boys of tyrants and of cities?
  My mother, you say, will go to Odysseus' palace.

---

37. Agamemnon was son of Atreus.

38. Laertes' son is Odysseus. Hecuba is to be a slave to Penelope, who in Homer's *Odyssey* has two elderly slave women whom she trusts and respects, Eurycleia and Eurynome.

39. "Class of men" means heralds, who delivered messages between city-states, even those at war, under immunity (they were under the protection of the god Hermes). Several Euripidean characters make hostile comments about heralds.

What about Apollo's prophecy
that she'll die here? The rest I will not mention—
I won't give voice to scandals and reproaches.[40]

Poor man, he doesn't know the suffering   450
in store for him. My troubles, and the Phrygians',
will seem like gold to him before he's done.
After ten years (on top of these years here)[41]
he'll come back to his fatherland alone

. . . .

where terrible Charybdis haunts the narrows[vi]   455
between the rocks; he'll face the mountain-dwelling
Cyclops—eater of raw flesh—and Circe,
Ligurian charmer who changes men to swine,
and shipwreck in the salty waves, desire
for Lotus, and Helios' undefiled cattle   460
whose bloody flesh will seem to have a voice,
a bitter message for Odysseus!
I'll make this short: he'll go, alive, to Hades,
and then, when he's escaped the deep sea waters
he'll find ten thousand troubles back at home.   465

(Cassandra begins speaking in trochaic tetrameters.)

Tell me, though, what *is* the point of standing here and letting
                                                    fly
prophecies? Forget about the struggles of Odysseus.
Let's go right away; I'll meet my bridegroom in the
                                                    Underworld.
Evil man, whose deeds appear so high and mighty, you will be
buried shamefully at night, great warlord of the Grecian host!   470
As for me, my naked corpse, cast into a ravine, will ride
swollen rills of snowmelt, past my bridegroom's resting place,
                                                    until
feral dogs discover it and tear apart Apollo's servant.

---

40. Cassandra alludes to the story of Hecuba's metamorphosis into a dog and death near Troy (explicitly foretold at *Hecuba* 1319 ff.).

41. Here (450–65) Cassandra briefly summarizes Odysseus' wanderings in the *Odyssey*.

Emblems of my frenzy for the god I love, farewell, farewell!
475   Festivals I reveled in, I've left you far behind; the breeze
sweeps away the garlands I have torn asunder from my brow.
While my body still is undefiled, I fling these gifts to you,
lord of prophecy. Where must I go now? Where's the general's
ship? Let's not waste time; keep watch! A breeze might come to
                              fill your sails.
When you take me from this land, you're bringing home one of
480   the three
Furies![42] Farewell, Mother; do not cry. Beloved fatherland,
brothers buried in the earth, and father who begot me, soon
you'll receive me; when I join the dead, I'll be victorious:
I will ravage my destroyers, wreck the house of Atreus!

(Talthybius escorts Cassandra off toward
the ships. Hecuba collapses.)

CHORUS: *(Among themselves.)*
485   Aren't you watching Hecuba? She's fallen
to the ground without a word, poor ancient thing!
Don't just stand there, lift her up! She's fallen!
She's an old woman—help her stand up straight.

(Members of the Chorus try to lift
Hecuba, but she waves them off.)

HECUBA:
No, girls—just let me lie where I have fallen.
490   Kindness that's unwanted is not kindness.
Falling down befits my situation:
the things I suffer now, and all I've suffered,
and all that I will suffer. O gods!—I know
the gods are worthless allies; all the same,
495   we call on them when evil fortune strikes.
It's what we do. So, first I want to sing

---

42. The Furies take vengeance for violations of divine law such as breaking
oaths or violence against relatives or guests. In tragedy, people who bring
destruction are often metaphorically Furies. Their number is not usually
fixed—Euripides may have made them three to make them resemble the
Fates.

of all the good things I have known; that way
I'll stir up greater pity for the sorrows.
I was royal, and married royalty.
The sons I bore were excellent: by no means   500
useless rank and file—they were the best
of all the Phrygians; no woman in the world,
Greek or barbarian, could boast of sons like mine.
I saw them fall, struck down by the Greek spear;
I cut this hair of mine beside their tombs,   505
and with these eyes of mine I saw their father
Priam, who engendered them, assaulted
and butchered at the altar of our home—
yes, I was right there, weeping, when he died;
our city fell before my eyes.
                The daughters   510
I raised in hopes of giving to distinguished
husbands, bridegrooms picked out specially—
I raised them (it now seems) for someone else.
They were taken from my arms; I don't expect
that we will ever see each other again.   515
And here's the capstone to my wretchedness:
old woman that I am, I will arrive
as a slave in Greece. They'll load me down with tasks
unsuitable for someone of my age.
I'll keep the keys, a servant in the doorway—   520
I, who bore Hector!—or I'll make their bread.
I, who had a queen's bed in the palace,
will rest my shriveled carcass on the ground,
my tattered body wrapped in tattered robes,
so shabby! I, who once was prosperous.   525
So much misfortune—all that I have been through,
and all that lies ahead of me—all this
because of just one woman and her marriage.

Cassandra, O my child, bound to the gods
by bacchic frenzy, circumstance has robbed you   530
of your chaste dignity. And you, poor thing,
Polyxena, where can you be? I bore
so many children; not a single one,
male or female, can help me. What's the point
of making me stand up straight? What do you hope   535

to accomplish? Guide these feet, which used to step
so delicately in Troy, to my straw mat
and to my rocky headrest on the ground
so I can fall down and exhaust myself
540   with tears. No one who hasn't gone down to death yet
can ever be considered blessed with fortune.

CHORUS:

[Strophe]

Sing to me, Muse, a new type of song:[43]
a tear-soaked dirge for Ilion.
Help me now to serenade Troy:
545   my tune will tell of the spears that took me captive:
the Achaean horse,
the four-legged wagon that brought my destruction
left outside the gates by the Argives
adorned with gold, enclosing within it the roar
550   that would reach high heaven, packed with armaments.
The Trojan people stood up on their rock
and shouted aloud:
"Come out, your struggles are over!
Let's bring this sacred statue
555   to Zeus's daughter, protectress of Ilion!"
What girl, what old man didn't rush out of doors to see it?
They sang out joyfully,
welcomed deception in, embraced their ruin.

[Antistrophe]

All of the Phrygians rushed to the gates
560   to fetch the polished mountain pine
ambush—belly swollen with Greeks—
a favor for the unbroken goddess,[44] mistress

---

43. This song is "new" for the Chorus because it is a lament for Troy,
which did not previously require lamentation, and because it introduces
typically Greek themes and poetic language into a Trojan song.

44. Athena is "unbroken" because she is a virgin. This imagery is frequent
in Greek poetry, but it is pointed here, since Athena is herself not "tamed"
but controls the horses of her war chariot.

of immortal foals;
they hauled Troy's ruin to shore like a black ship,
threw the linen cables around it   565
and drew it in; they placed it in Pallas's shrine[45]
as a gift for her. They cut the city's throat.
When darkness fell on their struggles, their joy,
the Phrygian tunes
poured forth from lotus-wood flutes, while   570
the maidens stepped in rhythm
and raised a shout with each stride, in a beautiful
and rich choreography, melody wrapped in movement,
as fire's black radiance
glowed in the hearth of every sleeping home.[vii]   575

[Epode]

I was at the temple then
singing and dancing in chorus
for Zeus's daughter, virgin of the mountains.[46]
A bloody cry went up in the city and held
Pergamon in its grip.[47]   580
Cherished babies threw their arms around
their mothers' robes in terror.
Ares was emerging from his ambush;
this was the work of the virgin goddess Pallas.
Around the altars, Phrygians were slaughtered   585
and from our deserted beds
the Greek blade that hacked at the necks of our men
harvested a garland of young girls
(who would nurture young boys in Hellas)
and left a raw wound in Phrygia.   590

(Enter Andromache holding her son Astyanax,
accompanied by Greek soldiers, on a cart piled with
the armor of Hector and other Trojan spoils.)

---

45. Pallas is Athena. In the *Iliad*, Athena has a temple on the citadel of
Troy, although she is implacably hostile to the Trojans.

46. This is Artemis.

47. Pergamon is properly the citadel of Troy, but the word often refers to
the whole city.

CHORUS:
Hecuba, look: it's Andromache, borne
on the foreigners' chariot. There in her arms
clutched to her trembling breast is her cherished
Astyanax, Hector's son. Where are you bound
595   in this wagon, poor woman, alongside the shining
bronze armor of Hector, and Phrygian spoils
that the Greeks hunted down and collected at spearpoint,
treasures of Troy that the son of Achilles
will take back to Phthia to garland their temples?

ANDROMACHE:

[Strophe 1]viii

600   The Achaean masters lead me away.
Alas.

HECUBA:
          You sing this paean; I composed it.

ANDROMACHE:
Ah, ah . . .

HECUBA:
                    . . . for this pain,
O Zeus, and this disaster.
My children, life is over now for us.

ANDROMACHE:

[Antistrophe 1]

605   All our wealth is gone, our city is gone,
poor Troy . . .

HECUBA:
                    . . . my noble children, gone away now.

ANDROMACHE:
Ah, woe.

HECUBA:
      Oh yes, woe.
My sorrows, and the city's
misfortune, as it smolders to the ground.

ANDROMACHE:
          [Strophe 2]

My husband, you should be here . . .   610

HECUBA:
You're calling to my child
in Hades. O poor man,
how can you keep your wife safe?

ANDROMACHE:
          [Antistrophe 2]

O bane of the Achaeans . . .

HECUBA:
O child, the eldest son   615
I bore to Priam, come,
carry me down to Hades.

ANDROMACHE:
          [Strophe 3]

Longing that tears us apart . . .

HECUBA:
        Every miserable anguish we suffer . . .

ANDROMACHE:
. . . all for a city that's gone . . .

HECUBA:
        . . . piling one pain on top of another.

ANDROMACHE:
Thanks to malevolent gods, when your child escaped Hades,
        he brought down   620

Troy's citadel—for the sake of a hateful affair, he destroyed
us.[48]
Corpses bespattered with blood lie in heaps alongside Pallas'
temple
waiting for vultures to take them. Troy was enslaved by his
actions.

HECUBA:

[Antistrophe 3]

Fatherland, desolate town . . .

ANDROMACHE:
As we leave you, I weep for my homeland . . .

HECUBA:
. . . here is your pitiful end.

ANDROMACHE:
625   . . . and my house, and my memories of childbirth.

HECUBA:
Children, we're going to be parted. Our city is empty, deserted.
What lamentation, what grief . . .
Tears follow tears . . .[ix]
Here in our home. But the dead can forget all the pain they
have suffered.

CHORUS:
630   Laments and tears, the Muse that sings of pain:
all these are sweet to those who suffer hardship.

ANDROMACHE:
Mother of Hector, whose spear once laid to waste
so many Argives, do you see all this?

---

48. Andromache alludes to the exposure of Alexander (Paris). The first
play in this production, *Alexandros,* dramatized how Paris, reared by a
herdsman, came to the city and was recognized by his family.

HECUBA:
I see the gods' work. They build up what's nothing,
and knock down what appears considerable.   635

ANDROMACHE:
My son and I are carried off as plunder.
From nobility to slavery—quite a change.

HECUBA:
Compulsion's force is terrible. Just now
they dragged Cassandra from me violently.

ANDROMACHE:
Oh god.
It seems your child must face a second Ajax.   640
But there's another illness that afflicts you.

HECUBA:
Oh yes—beyond all measure! I've lost count
of sorrows, one competing with the next.

ANDROMACHE:
Polyxena is dead. Your child was slaughtered
at Achilles' grave, a gift for a lifeless corpse.   645

HECUBA:
Oh no. That's what Talthybius meant. His words
were riddling, but now I see the truth.

ANDROMACHE:
I saw her, and I got down from this cart
to cover up her corpse, and beat my breast.

HECUBA:
Ah, this blood-offering was most unholy.   650
My child, how cruelly you've been destroyed.

ANDROMACHE:
She died the way she died. Still, I would say
she's luckier than I am. I still live.

HECUBA:
   Life and death, child, are two different things.
655   One is nothing. There's some hope in the other.

ANDROMACHE:
   In my opinion, never being born[x]
   is just the same as death, and I'd much rather
   die than live a life that's filled with pain.
   The dead no longer feel the sting of sorrow.[xi]
660   But when one falls from fortune to misfortune
   one's soul is exiled from its former joy.
   Polyxena is dead: she's unaware
   of her own misery; it's just as if
   she'd never seen the light—but I aimed high:
665   I had renown, then everything went wrong.

   I made an effort, when I lived with Hector,
   to practice wise restraint in every way
   a woman can. I avoided, first of all,
   the thing that causes a bad reputation
670   (whether or not blame is fixed on women):
   when a woman doesn't stay indoors.
   I set aside my longing, and I stayed
   at home. I did not open the palace doors
   to women and their clever talk; instead
675   my own mind was my guide—a worthy teacher.
   I kept a quiet tongue and placid eye
   around my husband. When it was important
   I claimed my victories, but I knew when
   I had to yield the victory to him.

680   The Achaean army heard about my ways
   and that is what destroyed me: now the son
   of Achilles wants to take me for his wife.
   I'll be a slave to my family's murderers.
   If I push my beloved Hector to one side
685   and open up my mind to my present spouse
   then I will seem unfaithful to the dead;
   but if I hate the man, I'll be detested
   by my own master.
                    Well, they say one night
   is all it takes to ease a woman's loathing

for a man's bed. I cannot stand a woman   690
who finds a new bed, loves another man,
forgetting all about her former husband.
Even a filly balks at pulling the yoke
when separated from her usual partner.
And yet a beast has no intelligence,   695
no speech—by nature, it's inferior.

Dear Hector, you were everything I needed:
a great man in your intellect, your family,
your wealth, your courage. When I was a girl
you took me from my father's house, a virgin,   700
and brought me to your bed; the marriage yoke
united us. Now you are dead, and I
am led off, captive, on a ship to Greece
where I will bear the yoke of slavery.

You're grieving for Polyxena's destruction—   705
aren't her sorrows less than what I suffer?
The one thing left for mortals to fall back on—
hope—I don't have even that. No one
has robbed my senses blind—I don't expect
to do well. I have no sweet misconceptions.   710

CHORUS:
The same disaster strikes you; your lament
instructs me where I stand in my own pain.

HECUBA:
I've never traveled on a ship myself;
my knowledge comes from hearsay and from pictures.
I've learned that sailors, when a storm at sea   715
is one that they can manage, are intent
on safety: one man takes the helm, another
is stationed at the sails, one checks the bilge.
But when the sea is wildly agitated,
too much for them to bear, they just let go   720
and ride the waves, wherever fortune drives them.
That's how it is with me. I have so many
griefs that I've let go. I have no voice.
This wave the gods have sent has overwhelmed me.

725   Beloved child, don't dwell on Hector's fate.
        Your tears cannot change anything; he's gone.
        Honor your present master; lure the man
        and win him to your side with pleasing ways.
        You'll bring your loved ones joy, and it may be
730   you'll raise my child's child to be Troy's greatest
        helper. Maybe one day your descendants
        will rebuild Ilion, bring back our city.

        (Hecuba sees Talthybius and attendants
        approaching from a distance.)

        But now I see that we must change the subject.
        A servant of the Greeks is on his way;
735   he has some new decision to announce.

TALTHYBIUS:
        Wife of Hector, once the greatest Trojan,
        don't hate me—I have come unwillingly
        to tell you of the common resolution
        of the Danaans and the sons of Pelops.[49]

ANDROMACHE:
740   What is it? Here's a prelude to bad news!

TALTHYBIUS:
        Your child . . . it was decided . . . how can I say it?

ANDROMACHE:
        Oh no—will he and I have different masters?

TALTHYBIUS:
        No Greek man will ever be his master.

ANDROMACHE:
        Will he be left here, a remnant of the Trojans?

---

49. The "sons of Pelops" are his grandsons, Agamemnon and Menelaus.
Pelops came from Lydia in Asia Minor, and referring to Agamemnon and
Menelaus this way is a reminder that Greeks and "barbarians" are not
essentially different.

TALTHYBIUS:
It's bad. There is no easy way to say it.   745

ANDROMACHE:
If it's bad, don't hesitate—just tell me.

TALTHYBIUS:
It's really bad. They're going to kill your child.

ANDROMACHE:
Alas; this news is worse than my forced marriage.

TALTHYBIUS:
Odysseus prevailed on all the Greeks . . .

ANDROMACHE:
Aah! This is terrible, beyond all measure.   750

TALTHYBIUS:
. . . that the greatest Trojan's son must not survive . . .

ANDROMACHE:
I hope that plan prevails for his own child!

TALTHYBIUS:
. . . but must be flung down from the towers of Troy.
Proceed as follows: this counsel seems much wiser.
Don't cling to him; grieve nobly for your sorrows,   755
and since you have no strength, do not suppose
that you have any power. Look around:
there is no safety for you anywhere.
Your city is destroyed, your husband's dead,
and you're defeated—we can certainly   760
hold our own against a single woman.
For all these reasons, please don't be in love
with conflict, or do anything that's shameful,
or anything that will create resentment;
don't fling curses at the Greeks. The army,   765
if your words make them mad, will not take pity
on this child, or allow him to be buried.
But if you handle your misfortune well,

if you stay quiet, you won't leave his corpse
770   unburied; you'll get more favorable treatment.

ANDROMACHE:
O dearest child, honored all too much,
You'll leave your wretched mother all alone,
killed by your enemies. A noble father,
for others, means security; in your case
775   it will mean your death. Your father's eminence
and goodness were, for you, inopportune.[xii]
My baby, are you weeping? Can you feel
these sorrows? Why do you clutch at me, and cling
to my robes, just like a little bird who's burrowed
780   under my wing? Hector will not come
back from beneath the earth, his glorious spear
in hand, to promise you security,
nor will your father's family, nor the Phrygians
in all their strength. You'll fall from a great height,
785   a desolate and pitiless descent,
and snap your neck; your windpipe will be smashed.
My precious little armful, dearest boy,
oh, the fragrance of your skin. It was
for nothing, after all, I swaddled you
790   and nursed you with my breast; your birth was all
in vain—the way I toiled, how much it hurt.
Now, for one last time, embrace your mother:
fall upon me, wrap your arms around
my back, and kiss my mouth.[50]
                                        O Greeks, devisers
795   of barbaric evils, why kill this child, who's done
nothing wrong? O Tyndareos' child,
you are not Zeus's offspring;[51] I can name
your many fathers: first, a Vengeful Curse,

---

50. Astyanax must be supposed to be too young to understand what the
adults are talking about (771–94).

51. Helen is Tyndareos' child because Andromache is sure that she was
not fathered by Zeus. Because Greek genealogical poetry, like Hesiod's
Theogony, includes abstract ideas among the gods, Andromache's imagined fathers for Helen are not so strange if Andromache sees Helen not as
a person but as a force of evil.

and then Resentment, Murder, Death, and every
evil that is nurtured by the earth.   800
I'm certain Zeus did not engender you,
the doom of so many barbarians and Greeks!
May you die! Your lovely eyes destroyed
the glorious plains of Phrygia. It was shameful.

All right, then, if it's been decided: take him,   805
fling him from the towers! Devour his flesh!
The gods are our destroyers; we cannot
protect this child from death. So, cover up
my wretched body, fling me onto the ship.
This is a lovely marriage ceremony   810
I'm going to, now that I've lost my child.

CHORUS:
Poor Troy, for the sake of a single hateful affair,
for just one woman, you lost tens of thousands.

TALTHYBIUS:
Come now, child, leave the loving embrace of your mother,
pain-wracked as she is, and ascend to the heights   815
of the garland of towers that crowns your ancestral
home; it's decreed you will breathe your last breath there.

(To his attendants.)

Take him.

      Announcements like this should be made
by a man who is pitiless, one who won't shrink
from shamelessness. I'm not the type for this business.   820

HECUBA:
O child, little son of my poor, pain-wracked son,
your life has been plundered away from your mother
and me. There's no justice. Ah, what will happen?
What can I do for you, unlucky boy?
I give you these blows to my head and my chest.   825
That is all I can do. Oh my city, alas,
what have we not suffered? What is there left
between us and immediate, total destruction?

*(Exit Talthybius, with attendants holding
Astyanax, toward the city; Andromache
is led on her cart toward the ships.)*

CHORUS:

[Strophe 1]

Bee-meadowed Salamis, island encircled by waves
830   so close to the sacred hill where Athena displayed
a spray of silver-green olive, her
heavenly garland, a gift, an adornment for glistening Athens;[52]
Telamon, ruler of Salamis,
you came here, you came from Greece
835   with Alcmene's son, the marksman,
long ago—questing for excellence with him—
to ravage Ilion, Ilion—our city, our home—

[Antistrophe 1]

then, when he first led the flower of Hellas to Troy,
when he'd been denied the foals that were promised to him;
840   he stayed his oar and he moored his ships
there by the Simoïs' beautiful streams,[53] bringing with him his
strong arm's
deadly aim, death for Laomedon.
He ravaged the land of Troy
with the blood-red blast of fire.[54]

---

52. Salamis, an island in the Saronic gulf off the coast of Attica, was politically part of the Athenian state. The song refers to the story of the contest between Poseidon and Athena to be the patron of Athens; Poseidon created a salt spring on the Acropolis, Athena an olive tree.

53. The Simoïs is the lesser of the two rivers in the Trojan plain in the *Iliad*.

54. King Laomedon cheated Poseidon and Apollo of their wages for building the walls of Troy. Poseidon sent a sea monster, which could only be stopped from destroying Troy if Laomedon's daughter Hesione were given to it. Heracles happened to pass by and offered to kill the monster in return for Laomedon's horses, a gift from Zeus. Laomedon agreed but reneged, and Heracles ("Alcmene's son" in 835) along with his friend Telamon of Salamis attacked and destroyed Troy.

Two times now, two brutal volleys subjected   845
the walls of Dardanus' city to their murderous spears.[55]

[Strophe 2]

It was in vain, as it turns out, your life on Olympus,
son of Laomedon,
your delicate steps among
wine cups of gold, your lovely   850
servitude to Zeus.[56]
Troy is in flames, your hometown.
The sea beaches echo
with dirges, cries—just like birds' for their young—
for spouses, for children, for mothers.   855
Your bathing places, sparkling with dew,
your exercise grounds, your racetracks,
all these have vanished, and yet
your untroubled expression
beside Zeus's throne maintains its grace,   860
lovely and youthful,
while Priam's land is destroyed by Argive spears.

[Antistrophe 2][57]

Eros, Eros, you who once came to Dardanus' palace,
you whom the gods cannot
forget; how you built up Troy   865

---

55. Dardanus, a son of Zeus, founded a city on Mount Ida and is an ancestor of the Trojan royal family.

56. Ganymede, a Trojan prince, was so beautiful that Zeus took him to Olympus as a cupbearer and beloved. Zeus gave his father (Tros or Laomedon in different versions) amazingly swift horses as compensation; these are the horses Laomedon promised Heracles.

57. This antistrophe deals with another myth about sexual love between a god and a Trojan prince: how the Dawn goddess fell in love with Tithonus, son of Laomedon. In the usual story, she asked Zeus to make him immortal but forgot to ask for eternal youth, so that he shriveled away. Here, however, the point is the gods' failure to care for Troy in return; we could compare Hecuba's argument at *Hecuba* 851–63 that Agamemnon should help her obtain vengeance because her daughter is his "wife" (concubine).

then, what a bond you fastened,
linking us with gods!
I will no longer blame Zeus.[58]
The warm light of white-winged
870   Heméra[59] glanced like a blade on our land's
destruction, on Troy's dissolution;
her children's father came from this place
and yet she looked on. A golden
chariot blazing with stars
875   swept him up to her bedroom;
his country had such high hopes for him.
All of the love charm
that Troy once used to enchant the gods is gone.

(Enter Menelaus with attendants.)

MENELAUS:
O lovely radiance of this day's sun!
880   Today I'll be the master of my wife.[xiii]
I came to Troy not so much for her sake
(as people think) but—more—to get back at
the man who—when he was my guest!—abducted
my wife, deceived me, when I was his host!
885   Thank the gods, that man has paid the price
and his land has fallen to the Hellenic spear.
I've come now for the Spartan (I don't like
to use her name, though she was once my wife).
She's somewhere in the captives' quarters, counted
890   with the other Trojan women. Those whose spears
toiled for her have given her to me
to kill, or (if I'd rather) bring her back
alive to Argos. It seemed best not to worry,
as long as we're in Troy, about the fate
895   of Helen, but to put her on a ship
and bring her back to Hellas; once we're there,

---

58. For not saving Troy for the sake of Ganymede. The women are going to blame Dawn instead.
59. Heméra is Day, here standing for Dawn.

I'll kill her, and her death will be the blood-price
for all of those whose loved ones died in Troy.[60]

And now, attendants, go inside and get her.　　　　　　900
Drag her out here by her murderous hair.
As soon as the winds are blowing in our favor
we shall escort this woman back to Hellas.

(Exit attendants into the tent.)

HECUBA:　　*(Raising her hands in prayer.)*
O you who hold the earth, and have your throne
upon it: Zeus, whoever you may be,
so hard for us to understand—compulsion　　　　　　905
of nature, or the mind that dwells in mortals—
I pray to you. You tread a silent path
as you direct mankind's affairs toward justice.

MENELAUS:
These prayers you make are very new and strange.[61]

HECUBA:
I praise you, Menelaus, if you plan　　　　　　910
to kill your wife. Be careful, though, and don't
look at her: desire is her weapon,
and she's hell-bent[xiv] to take you in; she takes
men's eyes, she takes down cities, burns down houses.

---

60. According to the lost epic, the *Little Iliad,* Menelaus was about to kill
Helen when she pulled aside her clothing; he relented at the sight of her
breasts. Helen returned to Sparta with Menelaus and lived peacefully ever
after. The audience would have suspected that Menelaus was unlikely to
carry out the plan he announces.

61. Menelaus' comment directs the audience to notice Hecuba's unusual
prayer. Zeus does not normally have his throne on the earth, but the philos-
opher Diogenes of Apollonia argued that air is the underlying constituent
of matter and holds the earth. Considering the possibilities that what
people call "Zeus" is really a natural order or is the same thing as human
thought, Hecuba combines a traditional form of prayer with the ideas of
philosophers like Anaxagoras and Diogenes. While Aeschylus had already
introduced contemporary thought into tragedy, Euripides does this often,
and sometimes, as here, draws attention to the resulting inconcinnity.

915   These are her enchantments. I know her,
          and so do you, and so do those who've suffered.

              (*Attendants emerge from the tent, leading
              Helen, who is sumptuously dressed.*)

HELEN:
          This is a frightening prologue, Menelaus—
          strong-armed by your attendants, and escorted
          by force from our quarters. I am fairly sure
920   you hate me; still, I want to ask: what have
          you and the Greeks decided? Will I live?

MENELAUS:
          No clear-cut ruling has been made. The army
          entrusted you to me, so I can kill you.
          I am the injured party.

HELEN:
                              Would it be
925   allowed for me to have a turn to speak,
          to argue that my death would be unjust?

MENELAUS:
          I came to kill you, not to talk it over.

HECUBA:
          Let her speak her piece; don't let her die
          without that opportunity, Menelaus.
930   But then, give me the chance to speak against her.[62]
          You don't know how bad it was in Troy.
          The entire story, when it's told, will leave her
          nowhere to run—the simple facts will kill her.

MENELAUS:
          The gift that you're requesting is my time.
935   All right, then: let her speak. It is allowed.

---

62. Hecuba's request informs the audience that a debate, an *agôn,* will
follow. Such formal debates are characteristic of Euripides.

But you should realize I'm granting this
because *you* ask, and not at all for her sake.

HELEN:
   I know that, whether I speak well or badly,
   you may not answer; you consider me
   your foe.[63] For my part, I'll take up the charges   940
   I think you're going to make, and answer them.[xv]

   First of all, this woman was the source
   of all our sorrows: she gave birth to Paris.
   Secondly, the old man is to blame
   for Troy's destruction, and mine: he didn't kill   945
   the baby—in the bitter image of
   a firebrand!—who was then called "Alexandros."[64]

   Now, listen: here's what happened after that.
   Three goddesses convened; he judged among them.
   The gift that Pallas offered Alexandros   950
   was to lead a Phrygian army and lay waste
   to Hellas. Hera promised him dominion
   over Asia and the lands within the boundaries
   of Europe, if he favored her.[65] But Cypris,
   smitten with my beauty, promised Paris   955
   me, if he judged her the loveliest.
   The outcome was that Cypris was the winner
   and thus my marriage benefited Greece:
   you haven't been subjected to the spear
   or to the rule of barbarians.   960
   Lucky for Hellas! But I was ruined by it:

---

63. Helen's opening is based on the requests for a fair hearing with which speakers in Athenian courts often began.

64. Before Paris' birth, Hecuba dreamed that she gave birth to a firebrand. Fearing the omen, Priam exposed the baby, but Paris was found and reared by a shepherd. He was named "Alexandros" ("defender against men") by the shepherds because he fought off bandits. It is not clear whether the "old man" is Priam or the herdsman who rescued the baby.

65. We do not know exactly what the bribes offered by Hera and Athena were in earlier versions. Probably Hera offered kingship and Athena military glory, but it is unlikely to have been traditional that they offered specifically rule over or conquest of Greece.

sold for my beauty, and now I am reproached
by those who should have crowned my head with garlands.
You'll say I haven't yet addressed the point
965   at hand: the way I left your home in secret.

The man who proved a vengeful Curse to *her*—

    (Indicating Hecuba.)

whether you call him Paris or Alexandros—
had with him when he came a goddess no one
can afford to underestimate. But you—
970   you really are the worst!—hopped on a boat,
sailed off to Crete, and left him in your home![66]
Ah, well.
For this next point, I ask myself, not you:
Why did I do it? I was not insane,
and yet I left home with a foreigner
975   (your guest!), betrayed my fatherland and household.
Go punish Aphrodite—then you'll be
more powerful than Zeus! He rules over
all the other gods, but he is slave
to her. I think that *I* can be forgiven.
980   Now, here's a specious point that you might raise:
when Alexandros died, and went below
the earth, my marriage—the god's own handiwork—
was over, so I really should have left
the house and gone to join the Argive ships.
985   I tried to do just that. As witnesses
I call the watchmen at the walls and towers:
they often caught me trying to escape
on a braided rope slung from the battlements.
My new husband Deiphobus[67] restrained me
990   by force—the Phrygians would have let me go.
How, then, would it be just for me to die
at your hands, my husband? How would that serve justice?[xvi]

---

66. In the epic *Cypria*, Menelaus went to Crete while Paris was his guest, leaving Helen to take care of him.

67. Deiphobus, a son of Priam and Hecuba, married Helen after Paris was killed.

He forced me into marriage, and I gained
bitter enslavement as my victory prize!
If what you want is to overpower the gods,   995
then you're a fool.

CHORUS:
                    My queen, defend your children
and fatherland! It's up to you to rip
her argument to shreds. She's so persuasive;
she speaks well, but she's evil. She's a terror.

HECUBA:
First of all, I'll prove myself an ally   1000
of the goddesses, exposing the injustice
in what she said. I don't believe that Hera
and Pallas Athena have so little sense
that they would put the cities that they love
up for sale—Argos handed over   1005
to barbarians, or Athens enslaved to Phrygia—
never!
          What would bring them to Mount Ida:
a beauty contest? Would they go play dress-up
like little girls?xvii Is Hera so in love
with glamour? Why? To get a better husband   1010
than Zeus? And was Athena hunting down
a mate—the goddess who implored her father
to let her stay a virgin, free from wedlock?

You shouldn't try to burnish your own faults
by claiming that the goddesses are fools.   1015
I doubt that you'll persuade the wise. You say
that Cypris came to Menelaus' house
together with my son. Oh, that's a laugh!
Couldn't she have moved you, and the whole
population of Amyclae,68 to Troy   1020
without ever leaving heaven? When you saw
my son, whose beauty was incomparable,

---

68. Amyclae, a village in classical times but important in the Bronze Age
and associated in mythology with Helen's brothers, Castor and Polydeuces,
was just south of Sparta and here stands for Sparta.

your own mind was your Aphrodisiac!
Yes, "Aphrodite" is another word
1025 for all of human idiocy. No wonder
the letters of her name can also spell
"atrophied"—she atrophies the brains[xviii]
of fools. You saw his clothing, bright with gold;
his barbarian finery was enough to drive
1030 you out of your mind. In Argos,[69] you made do
with little, and you hoped that you could trade
Sparta for our Phrygian town—already
awash in gold!—and make it overflow
with your extravagance. Menelaus' palace
1035 was not outrageously luxurious
enough for you.[70] Ah, well. You say my son
used force to take you. Did anyone in Sparta
observe this? Did you cry out loud for Castor
to save you, or his twin? They were still there,
1040 not yet among the stars.[71] You came to Troy,
the Argives hard upon your heels; the contest
of spears was under way, and men were falling.
If you received reports that Menelaus
was winning, you would praise him, just to taunt
1045 my son, to cause him pain, to make him think
that he had a great rival for your love.
But if the Trojans had the upper hand,
this man was nothing. Fortune guided you
in everything; you never chose to follow
1050 excellence instead. We kept you here
against your will, you say: you tried escaping,
throwing braided ropes down from the towers.

---

69. "Argos" here means Greece.

70. In the *Odyssey* (4.71–75), Telemachus is dazzled by the splendor of Menelaus' palace, which he compares to Zeus' house on Olympus.

71. Helen's brother Castor was mortal, Polydeuces immortal, but when Castor was killed (after Helen had gone to Troy), Polydeuces shared his immortality, so that they were dead one day, on Olympus the next (Pindar, *Nemean* 10 and *Pythian* 11). Euripides is the first surviving author to put them among the stars (they were identified with the constellation still called Gemini, "Twins").

I don't recall that you were ever caught
trying to knot a rope around your neck
or sharpening a dagger! Don't you think   1055
a noble woman would respond that way
if she were longing for her former husband?
And yet, quite often I advised you: "Daughter,
depart from here! My sons will marry others.
I'll help you, I'll escort you to the ships   1060
myself! Please, save the Greeks, and us, from battle!"
You wouldn't listen; my suggestion was
a bitter pill that you refused to swallow.
The life you led in Alexandros' house
was outrageous: you expected adoration,   1065
you wanted to see barbarians bow down
before you—yes, that meant the world to you![72]

And after all you've done, you step outside
dressed up so beautifully, and stand right there
before your husband, look him in the eye.   1070
I spit on you; you're an abomination.
You should have come out humbled, dressed in rags,
shaking with fear, your head shaved—all the wrongs
you've done up to this point should make you want
to show a little wise restraint, instead of   1075
this shamelessness.
                    Menelaus, here is my
conclusion: kill this woman, and you'll crown
the brow of Greece with victory. This act
is worthy of you. Make her an example
to other women; lay this down as law: 1080
if you betray your husband, you will die.

CHORUS:
    Menelaus, show that you are worthy
    of your house, your ancestors, and make your wife
    pay the price! Remove the blame that Greece
    has laid on women; your nobility   1085
    will shine forth as your enemies look on.[xix]

---

72. Greeks knew prostration as a Persian custom and abhorred it.

MENELAUS:
Your reasoning and mine have coincided:
she went from my house to a stranger's bed
willingly; she brings in Cypris now
as a way of boasting.

    (To Helen.)

1090   Go and find the men
who will stone you; let your death be a requital
however small, for the endless toil and struggles
of the Achaeans. You'll learn not to disgrace me.

HELEN: *(Grasping Menelaus' knees in supplication.)*
Don't kill me, by your knees; forgive me, please!
1095   The gods sent this affliction; don't blame *me*.

HECUBA:
This woman killed your comrades; don't betray them!
I beg you for their sake, and for their children's.

MENELAUS:
Old woman, that's enough. I pay no mind
to her. I ask my servants to convey her
1100   to the ships' sterns. From there, she'll go by sea.

HECUBA:
Take care that you don't sail in the same vessel.

MENELAUS:
Strange advice. Why not—has she gained weight?[73]

HECUBA:
A man in love will stay in love forever.

MENELAUS:
Depending on the beloved's state of mind.

---

73. Menelaus makes a joke that warns the audience that he is not recognizing his own vulnerability to Helen.

So be it—as you wish. She will not go   1105
in the same boat with me. Yes, you have a point.
When she arrives in Argos—evil woman—
she'll meet the evil death that she deserves.
She'll send this message to all of womankind:
Practice wise restraint.
                         This is not easy.   1110
But her destruction will frighten others—even
the more shameful ones—out of their idiocy.

> *(Exit Menelaus and attendants,*
> *escorting Helen to the ships.)*

CHORUS:

[Strophe 1]

Zeus, how could you? The fragrant smoke
that rose from Ilion's altars,
the bright flame, batter sizzling in oil,[74]   1115
clouds of myrrh in the air: all this
you betrayed—sacred Pergamon,
Ida's glades green with ivy, snow
that melts into streams and rushes down
the mountain's sides, the eastern edge that's struck   1120
by the dawn's first rays each morning—
our home. Our luminous, hallowed land.

[Antistrophe 1]

Gone now, all of your offerings;
the reverent shouts of the chorus
as night came, and they danced for the gods   1125
till the dawn; all the Phrygians'
golden statues; the hallowed moons[75]
(twelve in number)—all these are gone.
My lord, do you care? I'd like to know,

---

74. A mixture of ground grain, honey, and oil was a standard form of offering.
75. We do not know whether the "moons" are a crescent-shaped cake offered in sacrifice, or a ritual for the new moon.

1130   I'd like to know. You sit upon your throne
in the heavens, high above us,
while blinding flames take the city down.

[Strophe 2]

O my husband, you have perished
and you wander, my dear friend,
1135   unburied, your corpse never washed.
And I'll be sent away, shipped overseas
in a vessel that darts through the waves on its wings
to Argos' pastures, where the people live
behind Cyclopean walls, stones piled to the sky.[76]
1140   Our children stand beside the gates, too many to count,
streaming[xx] with tears, they cry, they cry:
"The Achaeans, Mother, are taking me away;
all by myself—you won't see me anymore!—
on a dark ship
1145   bound for sacred
Salamis, or for the peak
there at the isthmus, the steep
double lookout that stands high above
the portal to Pelops' domain."[77]

[Antistrophe 2]

1150   May the bark of Menelaus
in the middle of the sea
be struck down its center by fire—
the sacred bolt that Zeus hurls with both hands—
as I'm taken away, all in tears, from my land
1155   from Ilion, to be a slave in Greece,
while she lifts the golden mirror up to her face,

---

76. Euripides several times refers to the legend that the Cyclopes built the massive walls of Mycenae, Agamemnon's home. Although the wild and brutal Cyclopes of the *Odyssey* are more familiar now, Greeks alternately imagined the Cyclopes as powerful craftsmen who constructed thunderbolts for Zeus.

77. This refers to Acrocorinth, a twin-peaked hill that dominates the southern end of the narrow Isthmus of Corinth, which links the Peloponnese to the rest of the mainland.

delighting in it like a girl—the daughter of Zeus.
May he not ever reach his home
back in Sparta; may he not see his fatherland
ever again, or his hearthstone, or the town   1160
of Pitane,[78]
or the goddess
dwelling in gates made of bronze![79]
He made a marriage of shame
that was hell for great Hellas, and harm   1165
for Simoïs' beautiful streams.

> *(Enter, from the direction of the city,*
> *Talthybius and attendants carrying the*
> *body of Astyanax on Hector's shield.)*

CHORUS:
Oh no, oh no.
How our fortunes keep changing—each turn for the worse,
more bitter, more strange.
O unhappy wives of the Trojans, behold:
the Danaans are bringing the corpse of Astyanax   1170
whom they flung from the towers like a discus.

TALTHYBIUS:
There's just one ship still waiting, Hecuba:
it's loaded up with the remaining spoils
belonging to Achilles' son; it's ready
to sail to Phthia. Neoptolemus   1175
himself has left already. He got word
that Peleus was facing strange new troubles;
Acastus, Pelias' son, has cast him out
of his own country.[80] Rather than indulge
in any delay, Neoptolemus is gone;   1180

---

78. Sparta had five districts; Pitane was the most important, containing
the civic center.

79. There was a famous temple of Athena in Sparta called the "Bronze
House."

80. According to Pindar (*Nemean* 4), Acastus ambushed Peleus (Acastus'
wife had falsely accused Peleus after failing to seduce him), stealing his
magical knife, but Peleus defeated him through the intervention of the

so is Andromache. As she set out
I couldn't stop crying at the way she spoke
to Hector's tomb, and wept for her fatherland.
She asked that this corpse receive a burial:
1185   your Hector's child, who fell down from the walls
and lost his life. She wants this bronze-backed shield—
which this boy's father carried into battle
to strike fear into the Achaeans' hearts—
not to be brought to Peleus's hearth
1190   nor to the bedroom where she'll be a bride[xxi]
but to be the child's grave, to cover him
in place of cedarwood and stone. She asked
that he be placed in *your* arms; you'd take care,
as much as you were able, to wrap the corpse
1195   in burial robes and garlands. Her master's haste
prevented her from giving him a grave.

As for us, as soon as you've adorned
the corpse, we'll cover it with earth, and then
we must set sail. Please carry out these orders
1200   as quickly as you can. I've freed you from
one toil already; as I crossed Scamander
I bathed the corpse and washed its wounds. So, now
I'm going to dig a grave for him. Together
we'll get this done, then board the ship for home.

HECUBA:
1205   Hector's rimmed shield—place it on the ground.
This is a painful sight for me.

        (*Talthybius and attendants set the
        shield on the ground, then exit.*)

                        Achaeans,
your self-importance far outweighs your sense.
What fear made you destroy this little child
in such a strange, cruel way? Were you afraid
1210   that one day he'd revive our fallen city?
Then—as it turns out—all your power meant nothing.

---

centaur Chiron. No source except this passage says that Acastus drove
Peleus into exile.

When Hector's spear held sway, and many others',
we still were dying. Now the city's taken,
the Phrygians have perished, and you're scared,
terrified of a baby! I cannot praise   1215
a man who fears what he has not thought through.

Your death was so unlucky, dearest one.
If you had grown up and experienced
marriage, and become a godlike king,
and then died for your city in your prime,   1220
you would have been blessed—that is, if anything
about a death like that can be called blessed.
But as it is, you do not comprehend
the things you've seen, the things you might have had.[xxii]
Poor child! The towers of Loxias, the walls   1225
that were your patrimony: how they've shorn
your scalp, so ruthlessly. The curly hair
your mother kissed, and fussed with: torn apart,
the shattered bone exposed, a grinning wound—
I will not cover up the ghastliness.[xxiii]   1230
Oh, your hands: so sweet, so like your father's,
but limp, detached from your small broken wrists.
Oh, your dear mouth. How you used to boast
as you clung to my robes:[xxiv] "O Nana, when you die
I'll shear a great big lock of curly hair   1235
from my head, and lead a gathering of friends
to salute your tomb."[81] O child, you lied to me.
It's I—an agèd woman who has lost
her city and her children—I who bury
you, though you are young—your wretched corpse.   1240
Alas for all the times that we embraced,
the times I cared for you, or watched you sleep—
all gone. What could a poet write one day
upon your tomb? "The Argives killed this boy
once upon a time, because they feared him."   1245
A shameful epitaph indeed for Greece.

---

81. Even in ancient Greece, a very small boy would probably not express
his love for his grandmother by promising her a fine funeral, but in tragedy
children often say what adults want them to think—it would be appropriate for Astyanax to bury Hecuba rather than the opposite.

Ah, well. Your patrimony's gone, but still
you'll have this bronze-backed shield to be your grave.

    (To the shield.)

Defender of great Hector's lovely forearm,
1250   you've lost the one who shielded you in turn.
The imprint of his body on your strap
is sweet, and oh, his sweat has left a mark
on the rim—the sweat that often would drip down
from Hector's brow when he would toil in battle
and press this shield against his beard.

    (To women of the Chorus.)

1255   Go now,
and bring adornments for this wretched corpse,
whatever you can find.

    (Some of the women go into the tent to find
    adornments, returning as Hecuba finishes speaking.)

                  Our fate and fortune
do not allow us any great display
of beauty. But you'll have whatever's mine.

1260   That man's an idiot who thinks that joy
can be unchanging. By its very nature
fortune jumps around dementedly.
No one ever really has good fortune.

CHORUS:
    Look, these women have returned; they're bringing
1265   adornments from the spoils of Phrygia.

HECUBA: *(Dressing and adorning the body.)*
    O child, your father's mother decks you out
with finery taken from what once was yours.
But this is not for any victory
in horsemanship or archery, which the Phrygians
1270   honor and pursue insatiably.[xxv]
That woman whom the gods detest withheld

all these things from you—Helen took away
your life as well, demolished your whole family.

CHORUS:[xxvi]
Oh no, oh no,
you've touched me, you've touched a raw nerve! 1275
You whom I used to call
the great lord[xxvii] *of my city!*

HECUBA:
I deck your body with this finery,
these Phrygian robes you should have worn to marry
the noblest girl in Asia.
      And you, dear shield, 1280
mother of a thousand victories
when Hector carried you, receive this crown.
For you die with him, yet you shall live on
since you are far more worthy of being honored
than the arms of clever, wicked Odysseus.[82] 1285

CHORUS:
Ah me, ah me.
The earth will receive you, child,
to the strains of bitter wailing.
Mother, give voice . . .

HECUBA:
     Ah, me.

CHORUS:
. . . to the dirge for the dead.

HECUBA:
     Alas. 1290

---

82. The arms of Odysseus are at this point presumably the arms of Achilles,
which were awarded to him after Achilles' death. Just as he convinced the
Greeks to murder Astyanax, he persuaded them to award the arms to
him instead of to Ajax son of Telamon (the greatest Greek warrior after
Achilles, not to be confused with his namesake, Ajax son of Oïleus).

CHORUS:
Oh yes, alas. You'll never forget this sorrow.

HECUBA:
I'll treat the wounds I can with bandages,
bad doctor that I am—I have no skill.
The rest, your father will attend to, there
among the dead.

CHORUS:
1295 *Now raise your hands and strike,*
batter your head, deliver
a volley of blows. Ah, woe.

HECUBA:
My dearest friends . . .

CHORUS:
What are you saying? Tell us, Hecuba.

HECUBA:
1300 The gods, as it turns out, meant nothing more
than hardship for me. Of all the world's cities
they picked out Troy to feel their special hatred.
We sacrificed in vain. But if some god
had turned Troy upside down and hidden us
1305 beneath the earth, we would have disappeared:[xxviii]
no song would tell our story, and the Muses
of future generations would not know us.

Go, bury his corpse now in his wretched grave.
He has the ornaments he needs—he's dead.
1310 I don't believe it matters very much
to the dead if they have lavish funerals.
That's just empty ostentation for the living.

(Some of the women carry off the shield
holding Astyanax's body.)

CHORUS:
Ah, ah!
O poor mother, the great hopes you had for your lives

have been ripped into pieces.
Poor child, you were born to a prosperous family   1315
but now you have died a terrible death.
Oh, oh!
Look up there, in the heights of the town—who are they,
these men waving firebrands?
Something new, something strange, some cruel disaster
is about to befall the city of Troy.   1320

(Enter Talthybius with attendants.)

TALTHYBIUS: *(Calling to the soldiers offstage, in the direction
            of the city.)*
You captains, who are stationed there to burn
this city of Priam: the time has come. Do not
be lazy, now, don't hold on to your torches,
hurl them! We'll demolish Ilion
and then we'll happily set out for home.   1325

(To the Chorus.)

And you (I'll make this quick; a single speech
will have two outcomes), children of Troy, as soon
as you hear the commanders' signal, one high note
blown on the trumpet, go then to the ships;
the Achaeans will transport you from this land.   1330

(To Hecuba.)

And you, old woman—fortune has been harder
on you than anyone—follow these men here.
Odysseus sent them (since the lottery
made you his slave) to escort you from your home.

HECUBA:
Ah, poor me. This is the final grief,   1335
the endpoint of my sorrows. I shall leave
my fatherland; my city's set on fire.
Come, slow old foot—it's difficult, but hurry:
I want to embrace my dear, unhappy city.

(Hecuba starts walking in the direction of the city.)

1340   O Troy, how you once blustered! You were great
        among the barbarian peoples. Soon enough
        your glorious name will vanish. They're already
        burning you, and leading us away
        as slaves. O gods!
                            Why should I call on them?
1345   I've called the gods before; they didn't listen.

            (Hecuba breaks into a halting run.)

        I'll run into the pyre. That would be
        the finest way to die: in flames, with my homeland.

TALTHYBIUS:
        Poor woman, you're possessed. Your suffering
        has driven you insane.

            (To the attendants.)

                            Come on now, hurry:
1350   we must deliver her into Odysseus' hands.
        He's waiting for her; she's his prize of honor.

            *(The men bring Hecuba back; she and
            the Chorus sing a lament.)*

HECUBA:
                    [Strophe 1]

        Otototototoi.[83]
        Son of Cronus, prince of Phrygia,
        How can Dardanus' people deserve this?[xxix]
1355   Father of our race, do you see what we suffer?

CHORUS:
        He sees. But Troy does not exist;
        the great city is no city now.

---

83. This is a conventional way in tragedy of expressing a cry of grief.

HECUBA:

[Antistrophe 1]

Ototototoi.
Walls and timbers blaze, the rooftops
burn, and break in the fire. O my city   1360
Ilion, O Pergamon, flaring to ashes.

CHORUS:

Like smoke upon the breeze's wing
our land falls on the spear, and is gone.^{xxx}

HECUBA:

[Strophe 2]

O earth, my country, land that nursed my children.

CHORUS:

Oh sorrow, sorrow.   1365

HECUBA:

O children, listen, hear your mother's voice.

CHORUS:

All your lamentation's
useless—they are dead.

HECUBA:

Yes, and I call to them, falling to the ground,
striking the earth with both of my withered old hands.   1370

> *(Hecuba and the Chorus fall to their knees
> and beat the ground with their hands.)*

CHORUS:

And so do we—
we press our knees in the dirt
and call to our wretched husbands under the earth.

HECUBA:

We are led away, we're taken . . .

CHORUS:
                              Cry for pain, for anguish.

HECUBA:
. . . as slaves to our new station.

CHORUS:
1375   So far away from my homeland.

HECUBA:
Ah, ah! O Priam, Priam:
you are destroyed, you are friendless,
you lie unburied, you cannot see our ruin.

CHORUS:
Unholy slaughter brought dark, holy death
1380   to cover up his eyes.

HECUBA:
                              [Antistrophe 2]

O temples of the gods, beloved city . . .

CHORUS:
Oh sorrow, sorrow.

HECUBA:
. . . you feel the spearpoint, and the killing flame.

CHORUS:
Soon enough you'll crumble,
1385   nameless, to the earth.[84]

HECUBA:
Dust will go spiraling up like wings of smoke
into the sky, to keep me from seeing my home.

---

84. The Chorus are wrong; Troy, though destroyed, was remembered and
Greek inhabitants of the area associated themselves with it.

CHORUS:
  This land will lose
  its name; now everything's gone,
  flown off in every direction. Troy is no more.   1390

HECUBA:
  Do you hear that? Listen, listen!

CHORUS:

                              Pergamon has fallen.

HECUBA:
  The ground is shaking; shaking . . .

CHORUS:

                              . . . breaks like a wave on the city.

HECUBA:
  Ah, ah! My trembling, trembling
  legs, you must carry the footfalls
  that lead me on to my day of slavery.   1395

CHORUS:
  Oh, my poor city. But now it is time
  to board the Achaean ships.

          (Exit all to the ships.)

Endnotes and Comments on the Text

These notes include some comments on the language of the plays that may be of interest to all readers, but they are for the most part aimed at those who want to peek behind the editors' and translators' curtain at textual issues. This group includes not only students and scholars familiar with the plays in Greek, but anyone who wishes to study the plays in close detail, so I have tried to make the notes comprehensible to non-Greek-readers. Any reader may wonder, for example, what happened to the octopuses that appear in some other translations of *Hecuba* at 1162 Greek (1214 AS; see note xxxii).

Many verses that appear in our manuscripts have been suspected by editors of being interpolations, not written by Euripides but inserted later by actors, scribes, editors, or hacks. Modern editors use square brackets to indicate lines that they do not consider genuine; I have relegated such lines (where I agree with the deletions) to these notes and translated them for the sake of completeness, usually in such a way that readers or directors who feel they do belong in the text can reinsert them without disrupting the meter or syntax.

Some of Euripides' verses have been altered or garbled in the course of being copied and recopied over the centuries, and editors have proposed emendations, posited missing or copied-out-of-order lines, or, if a passage seems too corrupt to fix, marked the text with daggers or crosses. Such passages are discussed in the notes when they have a bearing on the translation, though of course I have not addressed every possible textual issue. For a brief account of the transmission of plays in the ancient world, see Csapo and Slater (1995), pp. 1–38.

A list of editions and commentaries cited by author's last name only appears at the head of the notes for each play; full references are given for these, and for any work cited more than once in the Endnotes, in the "Editions, Commentaries, and Textual Discussions" section of the Suggestions for Further Reading.

—DAS

Andromache

The following editions and commentaries will be cited by author's last name only: Diggle (1984), Garzya, Kovacs (1995/2005), Lloyd, Méridier, Stevens.

i. I omit the following line (7 in the Greek text): "than me has ever been or ever will be." The scholiast (ancient commentator) on this line says that it was inserted by actors who read the previous line to mean "now what woman more unfortunate . . ." See Stevens.

ii. The Greek text here (line 70) has a singular verb: *pepustai,* "[s/he] has found out," but the gender of the subject is not specified; it could be either Menelaus or Hermione. Editors have suggested various changes to the text to remove this ambiguity: Diggle accepts Ludwig Radermacher's solution of moving line 73 ("Menelaus / is after him. He's left the house already") to come before this line, making the subject of *pepustai* clearly Menelaus (L. Radermacher, *Observationes in Euripidem Miscellae* [Bonn: C. Georgi, 1891], pp. 9–10), and Stevens argues that this solution improves the train of thought. Kovacs accepts Johann August Nauck's emendation *pepusthon,* "[the two of them] have found out." I do not think that emendation is necessary; the ambiguity is more of a problem for a translator than it was for Euripides and his audience.

iii. I omit the following line (154 of the Greek text): "You women, then, I answer with these words" (Lloyd's translation). Since no one has yet spoken to Hermione, the verb "answer" (*antameibomai*) makes no sense. If this line is genuine, then some missing lines probably contained the Chorus' address to Hermione as she enters. See Stevens and Lloyd.

iv. There is a textual problem with line 195 of the Greek text. My translation follows Johannes Lenting's emendation (*tychêi d' hyperthei tam' eleutheran th' horais*), also accepted by Méridier.

v. K. H. Lee ("Euripides, *Andromache* 236ff," *Rheinisches Museum für Philologie* 118 [1975]: 187–88) proposes that this line and the previous one (251–52 Greek) were copied out of order at some point, and that they belong after 236 Greek (251 AS: "I say you don't, to judge from your own words"). This tightens up the dialogue, with Hermione immediately picking up on the word "sense" (*nous*); with the order of lines as they stand in the manuscripts and in my translation, she is picking up the word "sense" from five lines earlier (231 Greek, 246 AS). The transposition is attractive and Kovacs follows it. On the other hand, as Lloyd argues, 251

Greek (266 AS: "Say what I have come to hear you say") fits better in its traditional position.

vi. I omit the following line, 273 of the Greek text: "That's how bad we are, when we are bad." The note of a scholiast on 272 indicates that 273 was not in his text, and many editors have followed Carolus Gabriel Cobet in omitting it; the sense is complete without the line. A more literal prose translation: "a bad one [adjective agreeing with 'woman' in the previous line]; such a bad thing we are to humankind."

vii. In line 294 of the Greek, both Diggle and Kovacs accept Gottfried Hermann's emendation *moron* ("fate") for the manuscripts' *Parin* (direct object form of "Paris"). The latter seems to be an intrusive gloss explaining *nin*, "him": a commentator probably wrote *Parin* in the margin, and it was subsequently copied into the text, displacing another two-syllable word. A literal translation with the reading *moron*: "If only the one who bore him had flung him over her head—an evil fate." Since, as West (1980, pp. 11–12) points out, the meaning of 293–94 is complete without the word "fate," I prefer to translate with a more neutral emendation in mind: West proposed *gyna*, "woman" ("the woman who bore him"), and Davide Giordano proposed *pote*, "once" ("the one who once bore him"), a phrase with several parallels in Euripides ("Eur. *Andr.* 293s.," *Museum Criticum* 21/22 [1986–87]: 79–80). Willink (2005, pp. 189–90) argues that *moron* is needed for the sense.

viii. Andromache uses "deserve" in a double sense, as Stevens (p. 137) notes: "I consider you not good enough to be conqueror of Troy and Troy too good to be conquered by you." I omit the next two lines, 330–32 of the Greek text:

Outwardly, those who seem to have good sense
shine brightly; inside, they're the same as all men—
except in wealth. Wealth's very powerful.

Lines 330–31 are very similar to two lines quoted by the fifth-century CE anthologist Stobaeus, who attributes them to the fourth-century BCE comic poet Menander:

Outwardly some men seem to have good fortune;
inside, though, they're just the same as all men.

Stevens explains 330–32 as a parallel passage to 319–23 Greek (330–35 AS), which was copied into the margin and then, mistakenly, into the text at this point, where it is repetitive and ineffective. Stevens grants that line 332 ("except in wealth. Wealth's very powerful") "follows strangely after 331" (p. 137), and that Alfred Koerte, the editor of the fragments of Menander, does not regard it as belonging to the Menander quotation, but Stevens is reluctant to call 332 "a double interpolation." I suspect that 332 may belong in the Euripidean text, following on 329 Greek (342 AS) as Andromache's bitter acknowledgment of the one point of similarity between Menelaus and the great city of Troy.

Diggle brackets 330–33, and Kovacs condemns all of 330–51. Craik (1979, pp. 63–64) defends 330–33, and Kamerbeek in his 1986 review of Diggle criticizes the Oxford Classical Text editor's practice of "too rashly athetizing" in this play, citing the present passage among others. Kamerbeek's view is echoed by W. J. Verdenius in his review of Diggle (*Mnemosyne* 40 [1987]: 439–40).

ix. The word "conflict" here (362 Greek) is the Greek word *eris;* this word figures heavily in *Andromache* and is prominent in the first two choral odes (it occurs at lines 128, 295, 376, 489, 495, 508, 578, 667, 985 AS; 122, 279, 362, 467, 477, 490, 563, 644, 960 Greek). The goddess Eris (often translated as "Strife") is said to have played a part in causing the Trojan War, by initiating the competition among the goddesses that was then brought before Paris. See also note xii below.

The phrase "female conflict" (*gynaikeian erin*) is difficult here, since Menelaus' attack on Troy was motivated by a conflict *over* a woman, not a conflict *between* women like Hermione's quarrel with Andromache, and the Greek phrase cannot comfortably stretch to cover both cases. Stevens defends the manuscript reading, noting that a papyrus find supports it, but Diggle notes in his apparatus criticus that he would "almost rather delete" ("*delere paene malit*," p. 292) the last three lines of Andromache's speech (361–63 Greek), which according to the scholia were criticized by the Hellenistic scholar Didymus. See also Mueller-Goldingen (1987), pp. 216–19.

x. There may be a line missing between these two sentences (364–65 of the Greek text); see Diggle and Stevens.

xi. The Greek contains an additional verb whose meaning here is not agreed on. Lines 397–98 of the Greek read as follows: "But why do I lament these things, and not *exikmazô* and consider the things at my feet?" *Exikmazô* means "deprive of, or cause to exude, moisture," and is used metaphorically only here. For possible interpretations, see Stevens. The second verb, *logizomai,* which I here translate as "consider," has been used twice already in this play: at 126 Greek (131 AS) the Chorus tell Andromache to "be aware of" her misfortune, and at 316 (327 AS),

Menelaus tells Andromache to "think about" her choice between her life and her child's. Editors have found these two lines (397–98 Greek, 414–15 AS) problematic; Diggle follows J. A. Hartung in deleting them, noting in his apparatus, "these lines are either not genuine, or they are not in their proper place" ("*aut spurii sunt aut suo loco non stant*," p. 294); Kovacs follows Samuel Musgrave (who edited Euripides in 1778) in placing 397–98 where 404–5 (mid-420–422 AS) stand, and vice versa. Craik (1979, pp. 64–65) suggests placing 397–98 after 403 (419–mid-420 AS).

xii. In capitalizing "Conflict" I am following the suggestion of Willink (2005), who proposes solving the metrical problem in the manuscripts by substituting the phrase *erg' Eridos* ("the works of the goddess Eris") for the manuscripts' *eridos hyper*, "because of a conflict." See note ix above.

xiii. I am following Kovacs' text, anticipated by Reiske (see Kovacs [1980], p. 101 n. 26), with line 646 of the Greek text ("and those the Greeks gave credit for good sense") slightly altered and placed after line 647 instead of before it. There are problems with the logic and flow of the lines as they appear in the manuscripts:

How can old men be considered wise,
and those the Greeks gave credit for good sense?
Peleus, look at you: descended from
a glorious father, you formed a marriage-bond,
and yet you say things . . .

With the lines in this order, the text does not indicate with whom Peleus formed a marriage-bond (Stevens: "The ellipse is difficult," p. 174), and Menelaus is impugning the reputation for wisdom not only of old men but of anyone the Greeks have considered wise. As Kovacs (1980, p. 102) says, "the two [groups] are oddly lacking in parallelism . . . and the relevance of the second group to Peleus is never made clear." The alteration of the Greek is from *kai* to *kas*, a single-letter change to undo a correction that could have been made after the lines were copied in the wrong order.

Kovacs takes "those the Greeks gave credit for good sense" as a reference to Menelaus himself and his "command of the Trojan expedition, viewed elsewhere in the play as an elective office" (*ibid.*). Alternatively, it could be a reference to the marriage-bond that is Peleus' greatest claim to fame: his union with Thetis. The phrase "formed a marriage-bond" (*kêdos sunapsas*) closely echoes line 620 of the Greek (*kêdos sunapsai*, 637 AS: "I told my grandson not to form a marriage-bond / with you"); there the phrase refers to a groom's relationship to his father-in-law. Thetis' father is Nereus, who (like Proteus, another "wise old man of the sea") has the gift of truthful prophecy (e.g., Hesiod, *Theogony* 233).

xiv. As Lloyd (p. 139) points out, Menelaus' language becomes overheated here (652–53 Greek): "lit. 'fallings of corpses have fallen, falling by the spear.' Even taking into account Greek liking for aggregation of cognate words . . . this sounds bizarre. Menelaus is being bombastic."

xv. I omit the following lines, 668–77 of the Greek text:

> Consider this, now: if you gave your child
> away to some citizen, and she then endured
> this kind of treatment, would *you* sit silently?
> I doubt it. Yet you're kicking up a fuss
> for a foreign woman's sake, against the ones   5
> whom you should count as loved ones, by all rights.
> A man and woman both lament the same:
> a woman, when her husband is unjust;
> a man, whose wife at home is prone to folly.
> The man has bodily strength in his two arms;   10
> the woman trusts in parents and in loved ones.
> It's simple justice for me to favor my own.

These lines have been condemned by editors, following Hirzel, as an interpolation; see further Kovacs (1980, p. 102 n. 27). Page (1934, p. 65) calls them "an expansive interpolation, probably histrionic [i.e., made by an actor], specially written for this passage. Not so well composed as these are usually." The lines that I have numbered 7–11 above (672–76 Greek) are certainly incoherent and intrusive in this context, and there is some syntactic awkwardness in the Greek of lines 1–2 (668–69 Greek). Méridier and Garzya retain the lines.

xvi. I omit the following two lines, 701–2 of the Greek text:

> But they themselves [i.e., the people] are infinitely wiser,
> if boldness and decisiveness were added.

These lines were first deleted by Hartung as a suspected interpolation; Diggle and Kovacs follow Busche in deleting the previous two lines as well ("So high and mighty! . . . they are nobodies," 699–700 Greek, 716–19 AS). There is some awkwardness in the shifts from singular to plural in the Greek text ("high and mighty" translates the plural adjective *semnoi*), the transition from a military to a political context has been deemed intrusive, and the condition at 701–2 is clumsy.

xvii. On the attribution of this line (929 Greek) to Orestes (following the manuscripts), see Kovacs (1996), pp. 49–51.

xviii. Diggle and Kovacs delete this line (937 of the Greek text), following Nauck. For the linguistic objections, see Stevens.

xix. Neoptolemus is named only once in the play, at 14 AS. Here (line 972 of the Greek) Orestes refers to him as *ton de*, "the other one." The name Neoptolemus does not fit easily into iambic trimeter, and elsewhere in this play he is usually referred to by his relationships to others, e.g., "son of Achilles." On the high concentration of patronymics (used broadly to include all kinship terms) in this play, which goes beyond metrical necessity, see Susanna Phillippo, "Family Ties: Significant Patronymics in Euripides' *Andromache*," *Classical Quarterly* 45 (1995): 355–71.

xx. There are multiple textual difficulties in this ode, particularly in this stanza. It is possible, as Kovacs (followed by Willink 2005, p. 200) argues, that the trip of Orestes to Delphi ("the holy sanctuary") that the Chorus reference here is not the earlier visit in connection with his matricide but his current trip in connection with his planned murder of Neoptolemus. For different possible readings and interpretations of the Greek text, see Stevens, Lloyd, Kovacs (1980), pp. 38–43, and Willink 2005, pp. 196–204. Willink argues that the rare word *kelôr*, which I have translated as "whelp," is probably derogatory (p. 200, n. 48).

xxi. Punctuated differently, these lines (1115–16 Greek, 1157–58 AS) could mean, "The son of Clytemnestra was the one man who'd woven this whole strategy." Critics do not agree whether Orestes is present in Delphi as one of the attackers; for an overview of arguments, see William Allan, *The Andromache and Euripidean Tragedy* (Oxford: Oxford University Press, 2000), pp. 76–77. The lines "He felt the dagger blows / of Delphians, and the Mycenaean traveler" (1110–11 AS, 1074–75 Greek) suggest that Orestes is there in person; against this is the unrealistic compression of time, representing an extreme case of a tragic convention.

xxii. "For all the good it did him" translates the manuscript reading *all' ouden ênen*, "but he accomplished nothing" (1132 Greek). Diggle, following Borthwick (1970, pp. 15–21), reads "but they accomplished nothing." This creates a new problem of logic with the following *alla* ("but"), which Borthwick takes as "anaphoric" (p. 16), and Kovacs (1996, p. 53) reads *all' ouk anêkan*, "but they did not let up."

xxiii. Being at an altar, praying and making sacrifice to a god, should have protected Neoptolemus from attack. Compare Andromache's situation at the beginning of the play. Euripides uses the rare word *deximêlon*, "sheep-receiving," which I translate as "sacrificial," to describe both altars (129 Greek/134 AS and 1138 Greek/1183 AS).

xxiv. Diggle and Kovacs follow Hartung in deleting line 1151 of the Greek, "by a Delphian man who killed him." The text then reads: "The son of Achilles fell, struck in his side with a sharp sword [by the Delphian who slew him], but many others fell too" (trans. Kovacs). See Stevens and Lloyd. The rationale for deleting 1151 is that it provides pointless detail. In my view, the detail that others fell along with Neoptolemus would be less relevant than the detail that he was killed by the group effort of the mob (incited by Apollo's voice); the following lines show the importance of the crowd's unanimity against him. As Stevens notes, an ancient commentator provides the name Machaereus for the Delphian who killed Neoptolemus. Euripides may be nodding to tradition by mentioning a Delphian individual, but the focus here is on the crowd's action.

xxv. This responsive lament, a feature of many Athenian tragedies, is called a *kommos*. The Chorus speak lines 1233–34 (1184–85 in the Greek text), then Peleus sings the antistrophe. The responsive singing continues until 1272 (1226 Greek), when they chant in anapests to announce the appearance of Thetis. Spoken lines are interspersed: 1249, 1253–54, 1263, 1266–67 (1204, 1208, 1218, 1221 Greek).

xxvi. Since line 1251 of the strophe (1206 Greek) lacks a corresponding line in the antistrophe, either 1251 must be cut, or there is a lacuna (missing line) here, before 1265 (1220 Greek). Editors have taken both approaches. Most recently, Willink argues for a lacuna (2005, p. 207). The sense of 1264–65 AS (1219–20 Greek) seems to be complete, but there is a textual difficulty in line 1219 of the Greek, which may suggest that something is missing after all.

xxvii. John Jackson (*Marginalia Scaenica* [London: Oxford University Press, 1955], p. 51) realized that this line was out of place where it appears in the manuscripts (1254 of the Greek text, following 1302 AS: "And you, who shared my bed, will be rewarded"), and that it fits perfectly here. It was probably left out of one copy of the play (because its line ending is similar to that of the previous line), then added back in as a correction at the foot of the page, then reinserted out of order by another copyist who didn't see where it was supposed to go.

xxviii. I omit the following line, 1283 of the Greek text: "They'd never suffer hardship from the gods." This line was first deleted by Hartung, and Diggle, Kovacs, and Alan H. Sommerstein ("The End of Euripides' *Andromache*," *Classical Quarterly* 38 [1988]: 243–46) also condemn it as out of place here. The fifth-century CE anthologist Stobaeus cites a variation of this line, "They'd never suffer hardship in the end," as belonging to Euripides' *Antiope*.

Stevens, followed by Diggle, brackets the four preceding lines as well (1279–82, 1328–31 AS), but they are defended by Sommerstein and retained by Kovacs. See also Mueller-Goldingen (1987), pp. 226–29.

xxix. These last six lines (in chanted anapests) are also found at the end of four other plays by Euripides: *Alcestis, Helen, Bacchae,* and *Medea.* In *Medea* there is a small variation: the first line, 1415 (1464 AS), mentions Zeus the enforcer (cf. 169–70 [171 AS]) instead of "the deities." See also my notes on *Alcestis* 1228 and *Medea* 1469 (Arnson Svarlien 2007, pp. 194–95, n. xi).

Hecuba

The following editions and commentaries will be cited by author's last name only: Battezzato (forthcoming), Collard (1991), Daitz, Diggle (1984), Gregory, Kovacs (1995/2005), Matthiessen, Méridier, Tierney.

i. For this arrangement, see Nicholas Lane, "Staging Polydorus' Ghost in the Prologue of Euripides' *Hecuba*," *Classical Quarterly* 57 (2007): 290–95, arguing against the prevailing view that Polydorus' ghost appears on top of the *skênê* (scene building).

ii. Editors reject the following line, "Take me, carry me, send me along, lift me up" (62–63 of the Greek text), on grounds of faulty meter and sense.

iii. The meter here switches from chanted to sung anapests (see p. xxx).

iv. The authenticity of lines 76–78 AS (73–78 Greek) has been suspected, on grounds of style, meter, and content; among recent editors, Diggle, Kovacs, and Gregory delete. Matthiessen and Daitz retain the lines, with emendations to repair the corrupt final line. For full discussions of 73–97, see Kovacs (1988) and Bremer (1971).

v. These lines too have been suspected (88–89 AS, 90–91 Greek). Like 76–77 AS (73 f. Greek), they are dactylic hexameters, unusual in anapestic passages; as Matthiessen and Gregory (citing Erbse) argue, this supports rather than impugns their authenticity. Again, Diggle and Kovacs delete, and Matthiessen and Daitz retain. Gregory considers these lines genuine; see her note *ad loc.* Diggle, following Baier and Wilamowitz, further deletes 92–97 (90–95 AS) but notes in his apparatus criticus that he is hesitant ("*de 92–7 haereo*," p. 343).

vi. See Charles E. Mercier, "*Hecuba* 145," *Mnemosyne* 47 (1994): 217–20, for arguments in favor of retaining this line.

vii. Most editors delete the rest of lines 175–76 of the Greek:

> so you may know what kind, what kind
> of rumor I hear concerning your life.

Gregory and Matthiessen also delete "Oh my child" (167 AS, 175 Greek), but Diggle and Kovacs retain this phrase, since it appears in Aristophanes' parody of this lament in *Clouds* 718–19 and 1165–66, 1170. On the textual issues in this passage (146–209 AS, 154–215 Greek), see Collard, Gregory, Matthiessen, Bremer (1971), and Kovacs (1996), pp. 56–58.

viii. Polyxena's song (antistrophe, 189–209 AS = 197–215 Greek) corresponds metrically to Hecuba's song (strophe, 146–66 AS = 154–74 Greek). The intervening dialogue is also sung.

ix. The phrase that I've translated as "what . . . next" here (217 Greek) and at 82 and 169 AS (83, 177 Greek) is *ti neon,* "something new," which often has the euphemistic meaning "something bad."

x. I omit the following two lines (265–66 Greek):

> He should have asked for Helen as his victim,
> for she destroyed him, leading him here to Troy.

Kovacs makes a good case for deleting these lines as a stylistically flawed interpolation, "entirely within the capabilities of the dullest Byzantine schoolmaster . . . penning an explanatory mythological note in verse" (1988, p. 129); see also Kovacs (1996), p. 59, and Gregory. I agree that the lines spoil the rhetorical structure and point of what follows (268–69 AS, 269–70 Greek). For a defense of the lines, however, see Battezzato (2000–2001), pp. 225–26.

xi. In Greek, "I'm begging for *charis*" (276). *Charis* has a broad range of meaning, including delight, charm, and loveliness (as embodied by the Charites, the goddesses we call in English the Graces) and the obligation to repay favors. It is an important concept in Greek culture and the plays of Euripides generally, and, especially in the sense of reciprocal kindness and gratitude, it is prominent in this play. I translate *charis* as "favor" at 257, 884, 906, 933, and 1227 AS (257, 855, 874, 899, 1175 Greek), and as "gratitude" at 328, 398, 858, 1262 AS (320, 384, 830, 1211 Greek). I use both "favor" and "gratitude" to translate *charis* at 859–60, 1251, and 1302 AS (832, 1201, 1243 Greek). *Charis* is also the root of *acharistos,* which I translate as "ungracious" at 131 and 254 AS (137, 254 Greek). In

Andromache and *Trojan Women, charis* occurs more frequently as a preposition meaning "for the sake of," but I translate it as "favor" at *Trojan Women* 89 and 562 AS (87, 537 Greek), as "grace" at *Trojan Women* 860 AS (836 Greek), and with the ideas of "delight" and "reward" at *Trojan Women* 1157 AS (1108 Greek) and *Andromache* 1302 AS (1253 Greek).

xii. With the repetition of "counsels" (cf. 250 AS; in the Greek, *bouleumasin* at the end of lines 251 and 331) the debate ends where it began; this formal device, common in Greek poetry, is called ring composition.

xiii. Lines nearly identical to these (411–12 Greek, 427–28 AS) occur at *Alcestis* 207–8 (211 AS, with note ii). For the argument that line 412 (428 AS) does not belong in the text here, see Kovacs (1988), p. 130, Kovacs (1996), pp. 60–61 (pointing out that line 412 is missing from part of the manuscript tradition), and Franco Ferrari, "In Margine All'*Ecuba*," *Annali della Scuola Normale Superiore di Pisa* 15 (1985): 45–49. Most editors retain the line; Collard (p. 151) argues that the deletion, "with a stop after 411, is very awkward."

xiv. My translation follows the order of these lines (414–21 Greek, 430–37 AS) as they appear in Diggle's edition; in the manuscripts, 435–36 AS (415–16 Greek) follow line 430 AS (414 Greek). Diggle (1994), pp. 229–38, argues that there is a great improvement in the sense of the lines with this transposition; Kovacs and Collard follow Diggle. Gregory and Matthiessen retain the traditional order; see their commentaries. The traditional order is also defended by Kamerbeek (1986, p. 101) and by Mastronarde in his review of Diggle's edition (*Classical Philology* 83 [1988]: 151–60). Diggle's strongest argument, in my view, is the improvement if 421 Greek (437 AS) follows 416 instead of 420 (436 instead of 434 AS), so that "the verb to be supplied [at 421] is no longer *thanoumetha* ['I'll die'] but 'I shall live'" (1994, p. 232). The logical flow and rhetorical balance is improved with Diggle's line order, but the order found in the manuscripts is also plausible; with it, as Gregory argues, the lines represent "a dialogue in form only, as each woman, hitherto so responsive to the other, turns to the contemplation of her own fate" (p. 93).

xv. Euripides here takes up a play on words between Helen's name and the verbal root *hel-* ("take, seize, destroy") famously used by Aeschylus at *Agamemnon* 681–90. For a defense of these lines (441–43 Greek, 458–61 AS), deleted by Diggle and Collard, following Dindorf, see Kovacs (1996), pp. 61–63. See also the play on Paris' name at 975 AS below (945 Greek).

xvi. C. W. Willink may be right to argue that *pontias* ("of the ocean") here (444 Greek) is a textual corruption and that Euripides wrote *potnias* ("Holy One"), a title of respect for female divinities, in keeping with the hymnic style of the ode ("Euripides, *Hecuba* 444–6/455–7, *Helen* 1465–77, *Bacchae* 565–75," *Mnemosyne* 58 [2005]: 499–509). The repetition of "ocean" is inelegant to our ears (Willink calls it "somewhat frigid" *ibid.*, p. 499), but not necessarily alien to Euripides' lyric style; compare the repetition of "night" at 71–72 AS (68–69 Greek). In iambic dialogue passages, such repetition is rife; cf. Gregory's note on 501.

xvii. The Chorus are deluded not only about the kind of work they will do as slaves in Greece; they are also mistaken about the design woven into Athena's robe, which depicts the Gigantomachy (Athena's *aristeia*, her display of excellence in battle), not the Titanomachy (which took place before Athena was born). For the significance of their mistake, see Zoe Stamatopoulou, "Weaving Titans for Athena: Euripides and the Panathenaic Peplos (*Hec.* 466–74 and *IT* 218–24)," *Classical Quarterly* 62, (2012) 72–80.

xviii. Recent editors are unanimous in deleting the following line: "—false, supposing the race of gods exists—" (490 Greek, trans. Kovacs, with minor modification) as an awkward interpolation. The deletion was first proposed by Johann August Nauck.

xix. I omit the following two lines (555–56 Greek), rejected by most editors (following Jacobs) as a poorly worded and derivative expansion:

> And they, when they had heard his final word,
> released her, for his power was the greatest.

These lines are defended, however, by Werner Biehl, "Interpretationsprobleme in Euripides' *Hekabe*," *Hermes* 113 (1985): 257–66, and Daitz retains them.

xx. There is a play on words in the Greek here; Hecuba is called *pan-athlios*, "entirely wretched," and the subsequent language of the games (*nikôs', stephanon*, 659–60 Greek) points to the etymological connection between *athlios*, "wretched," and athletics. Hecuba is the champion of misery.

xxi. Some of Hecuba's lines in this section are iambic trimeter, the usual spoken meter. I have left them unitalicized to distinguish them from the sung lyric meters (italicized: mostly dochmiacs), but Hecuba's iambic lines here may have been sung as well.

xxii. At some point in the following dialogue, Hecuba throws her arms around Agamemnon's knees. See Charles E. Mercier, "Hekabe's Extended Supplication (*Hec.* 752–888)," *Transactions of the American Philological Association* 123 (1993): 149–60, arguing that Hecuba maintains her suppliant posture throughout 752–888 Greek (780–920 AS). As Gregory points out, however, the text indicates gestures on Hecuba's part, so Hecuba and Agamemnon are not "clinched immovably together" (*ibid.*, p. 158; Gregory, note on 751–53).

xxiii. I omit the following lines (793–97 Greek):

> We sat at the same table
> often; he was first among my guest-friends.
> I looked out for him; he got what he was owed.
> And then he killed—if that's what he wanted,
> then why not think him worthy of a tomb?
> Why throw him in the ocean?

These verses contain some problematic and difficult-to-construe Greek, and are deleted by most editors (Diggle, Kovacs, Collard, Gregory, Battezzato; see their commentaries), following Nauck, though Méridier (see his note), Matthiessen, and Daitz retain them. The most difficult locution is 796–97 ("And then he killed . . ."). Tierney notes on 796, *ei ktanein ebouleto* ("if he wanted to kill"): "This can only be construed by a rather violent ellipse 'assuming (that there might be some excuse for) his wanting to kill the boy (he might at least have buried him, but) he did not think him worth a grave.' The feeling is Greek, the language very peculiar." Page (1934, p. 68) considers the whole passage a badly written actor's interpolation. Collard and Kovacs (1987, p. 144 n. 51) attribute the lines to a copyist who wished to explain the reference to "the gods above or those below" at 791 Greek (821–22 AS).

xxiv. The text and meaning are uncertain here; see the commentators. My translation follows the text as emended by Busche, followed by Diggle, Collard, and Gregory, with "compulsion" (*anankê*) in the genitive (possessive) case. The manuscripts have the word in the accusative (direct object) case, which would mean "the laws determine necessities." Both readings pose difficulties of syntax or meaning in the Greek. Matthiessen marks the line as corrupt with the editor's "daggers of desperation." Battezzato conjectures *kainas anankas,* "the laws determine new (or unexpected) obligations."

xxv. Most commentators (Tierney, Collard, Gregory, Kovacs 1987 [p. 145, n. 57]) accept an emendation made by Peter Elmsley, *emoi* for *soi* (859 Greek), which would change the meaning to "if he is dear to me." Battezzato, however, defends the manuscript reading.

xxvi. The manuscripts have the redundant phrase *Troian Iliad'*, "the part of the Troad in front of Ilion" (Battezzato), "in effect 'Trojan Troy'" (Willink). Willink argues persuasively that *Troian* does not belong here, but it is uncertain what word it has displaced. He proposes *petran* ("the rocky citadel of Ilion"), which Kovacs adopts. Matthiessen adopts Burges' *patran* ("fatherland"). See Battezzato and C. W. Willink, "Text and Metre in Three Cantica of Euripides: *Hecuba* 905–22, *Ion* 763–803, *Bacchae* 402–33," *Mnemosyne* 57 (2004): 45–79, esp. 51–52.

xxvii. Euripides plays on Paris' name by adding to it a prefix that means "terrible," following the lyric poet Alcman in a tradition of name-play that goes back to Homer: with Euripides' *Ainoparis* (945 Greek), compare Homer's *Dysparis* at *Iliad* 3.39. Compare also the play on Helen's name at 461 AS (443 Greek), and in *Trojan Women* (913, 1165, 1277 AS, with notes xiv and xxvii).

xxviii. I omit the following line (974 Greek): "Polymestor—besides, there is a law." This is Battezzato's solution; see his commentary. The difficulty posed by 973–75 Greek is that Polymestor's response ("it's no wonder, really") does not follow well from Hecuba's appeal to a general social law. Kovacs deletes all of 973–75, Diggle 974–75.

xxix. Following Kovacs' text (1013 Greek). With Diggle's accentuation, the meaning would be: "Where? In your robes, or do you have them hidden?"

xxx. This choral passage (1023–34 Greek) is primarily in sung dochmiacs, which I have italicized, but also includes two lines of iambic trimeter (1024, 1032 Greek; 1053, 1063 AS), which were probably spoken. Cf. note xxi above, and see Battezzato's commentary on both passages.

xxxi. I omit the following line (1087 Greek): "some cruel god has given this to you." Most editors delete this line, following Hermann; the exceptions are Daitz and Matthiessen. It is almost identical to 723 Greek (cf. 748 AS), and in this context is less appropriate and syntactically awkward; see Battezzato's commentary *ad loc.* and Battezzato (2000–2001), p. 227.

xxxii. The text has been considered problematic here (1162 Greek) by several editors, to whom it seems pointless to say that the Trojan women are "like enemies" (*polemiôn dikên*). My translation of "like enemies" ("now / no longer friends, but wartime foes") reflects what I take to be the intended meaning. Diggle and Battezzato accept A. W. Verrall's conjecture "like octopuses" (*polypodôn dikên*).

xxxiii. There is a repeated, untranslatable play on the word *korai,* which in Greek means both "girls" and "pupils" (because of the tiny reflected image that appears in the pupil of the eye). Hecuba, Agamemnon, and Polymestor all speak of the *korai* of the eyes (1002, 1078, 1162, 1222 AS; 972, 1045, 1117, 1170 Greek). The Trojan women are called *korai* at 500, 1100, and 1199 AS (485, 1063, 1152 Greek). The singular, *kore,* is used to refer to Polyxena at 51, 217, 408, 541, 559, 590, and 755 AS (46, 222, 394, 522, 537, 566, 728 Greek). The remaining uses of this word in the play are all in the choral odes: the Delian girls at 480, the Laconian girl at 676, and the Dorian girl to whom the Chorus compare themselves at 967 AS (462, 651, 934 Greek).

xxxiv. I omit the following two lines (1185–86 Greek):

For we are many; some incur resentment,
others belong by nature with the wicked.

The lines as transmitted have syntactical problems, and their sententiousness (combined with their not-quite-appropriateness here) raises the suspicion that they are a marginal parallel passage mistakenly copied into the text (cf. Page [1934], p. 68, and Collard). Most editors delete, following Dindorf; Daitz repunctuates and emends; Matthiessen crucifies. The MSS reading is defended by Juan Antonio López Férez, "Consideraciones sobre el texto de la 'Hecuba' de Euripides," *Emerita* 45 (1977): 435–51.

xxxv. This line (1270 Greek) does not make good sense as transmitted in the manuscripts: "Dying, or living here, will I fulfill my life?" Diggle daggers the final word, "life" (*bion*), and most editors emend by replacing it with a word that means "prophecy" (*phatin*: Weil, followed by Kovacs, Battezzato 2010, and Matthiessen) or "fate" (*moron,* Brunck, followed by Gregory; see her commentary, and cf. Musgrave's *potmon*).

xxxvi. The text gives no indication of what happens to the bodies of Polydorus' sons; they may be left lying onstage. See Judith Mossman, *Wild Justice* (Oxford: Clarendon Press, 1995), p. 68: "It seems at least possible (we are not told of anyone removing them) that they are still visible at the play's end, abandoned like Polydorus, as their father feared they would be at 1075ff. [1119–25 AS]. If this is right, then the ending is bleak indeed."

Trojan Women

The following editions and commentaries will be cited by author's last name only: Barlow, Biehl, Diggle 1981a, Kovacs 1999, Lee, Murray, Parmentier 1925.

i. I omit the following two lines (13–14 Greek):

> One day it will be called the "Horse of Planks":
> its Plan was death throughout the Trojan ranks.

More literally, "Because of this, by men of a later time it will be called the Wooden [*doureios*] Horse, since it held a spear [*doru*] hidden within." The play on words was criticized as "frigid" by a scholiast (ancient commentator), and most editors (following George Burges' 1807 edition) do not consider these lines genuine. For a defense of their authenticity, see Léon Parmentier, "Notes sur les *Troyennes* d'Euripide," *Revue des études grecques* 36 (1923): 46–61, esp. 46–49, and Francis M. Dunn, "Beginning at the End in Euripides' *Trojan Women*," *Rheinisches Museum für Philologie* 136, no. 1 (1993): 22–35, esp. n. 23. Dunn argues that this etymology is one of several elements usually found at the end of a Euripidean play, but which in *Trojan Women* Euripides places at the beginning instead. See also note 10 in this volume.

ii. The meter here switches from chanted to sung anapests (see p. xxx).

iii. The Greek here (and at *Andromache* 459 AS) designates Sparta by saying "the Eurotas" (the river that flows through Sparta); cf. *Hecuba* 676 AS, and below, 223 AS.

iv. The manuscripts here (201 Greek) read "children's bodies" (*tekeôn sômata*) instead of "parent's house." Biehl and Lee accept the MSS reading; following Diggle, Barlow, and Kovacs, I translate the text as emended by Parmentier (*tokeôn dômata*), which involves a very small orthographical change and is better suited to the context.

v. I omit the following lines (383–85 Greek), which are fraught with problems of style and coherence:

> The army's worthy of this sort of praise.
> Disgraceful things are better met with silence;
> I wouldn't want my Muse to sing of evils.

Diggle and Kovacs, following earlier editors, delete these lines; Biehl and Lee retain them.

vi. Evidently one or more lines are missing before this line.

vii. The line at the end of the antistrophe (550 Greek) is two syllables shorter than its corresponding line in the strophe (530 Greek), so something is clearly missing. The original line apparently contained some form of the word "sleep," and some form (perhaps a compound) of the verb "gave" (with the gleam of the fire as its subject); editors have supplemented in various ways. I have included the idea of "sleep" in my translation, but we cannot be confident of Euripides' exact words at this point.

viii. In the first two strophe/antistrophe pairs of this song (577–594 Greek, 600–617 AS), I follow the line attributions (following Charles Willink) and text (following Willink, Kovacs, Musgrave, Seidler) as they appear in Kovacs' 1999 Loeb Classical Library edition.

Hecuba has no doubt risen to her feet by now, though the text does not indicate exactly where.

ix. Words are evidently missing from lines 627 and 628 AS (604–5 Greek), since the lines do not match their corresponding lines in the strophe (621–22 AS, 598–99 Greek). Strophe and antistrophe 3 are in dactylic hexameter, the meter of epic.

x. I omit the preceding two lines (634–35 Greek):

O mother who bore me, hear my lovely words:
my speech will cast delight into your mind.

Diggle and Kovacs, following Dindorf, delete these lines. Diggle comments in his apparatus criticus that "lovely words" and "delight" do not fit the context, and "mother who bore me" is absurd—Hecuba is Andromache's mother-in-law, not her mother. Andromache might address her loosely as "O mother," just as Hecuba called her "child" two lines earlier, but the elaboration makes no sense. Various solutions have been proposed, none of them satisfactory. See, e.g., Sansone (1983, p. 228), who proposes repunctuating to give the sense "O mother, bearer of the loveliest children." Sansone himself effectively puts to rest other proposals.

xi. This line (638 Greek) may mean something like this, but the Greek is difficult to construe and the text may be corrupt or have missing words. Diggle marks the line with daggers; Kovacs, following Seidler, proposes that two missing half-lines intervened between the first and second halves of 638.

xii. I omit the following four lines (745–48 Greek):

> O my luckless bed, and O my marriage,
> the child I bore to Hector in his palace
> was meant to rule over Asia's fertile grainlands,
> not to be cruelly slaughtered by the Greeks.

West (1980, pp. 15–16) argues for their deletion on the basis of problematic Greek in line 745, and the unmetrical (as transmitted) and inapt line 747; neither line has been convincingly fixed by emendation. West adds that this speech "is an emotional and rhetorical display piece that naturally invited interpolation."

xiii. I omit the following lines (862–63 Greek; if they were retained, they would be preceded by a comma rather than a period in my translation):

> Helen. I am Menelaus, who toiled
> long and hard—and the Achaean army.

A scholiast on these lines notes that the statement "I am Menelaus" is superfluous, since the audience would be able to identify Menelaus without it. This, along with the awkwardness of the syntax in the second line (reflected in my translation), led van Herwerden to delete these lines, and he is followed by Lee and Diggle. West (1980, p. 16) solves the problem of the awkward phrase "and the Achaean army" by positing that a copying error led to the loss of two half-lines between the first and second halves of 863 Greek. Kovacs, following West's suggestion, translates as follows (supplements are in angle brackets): "I, Menelaus who endured so many toils <in war and overthrew the city of Troy, am now> going <to Greece,> and the Greek army with me!"

The other objection to 862 Greek is that in it Menelaus names Helen, then a few lines later professes a distaste for saying her name and calls her "the Spartan" instead. West (1980, p. 16; cf. Biehl in his apparatus criticus) disregards this objection, pointing out that Menelaus does go on to name Helen at 877 Greek (895 AS): "The reservation [about using Helen's name] expressed in 869f [Greek; 887–88 AS] is invented *ad hoc* and has no validity outside that sentence." However, it is one thing to express reluctance to say a name, then spit it out nevertheless seven lines later; it is another to express such reluctance seven lines after one has already said it! The latter makes no sense rhetorically; the former is, I believe, what Menelaus does. Note the play on sounds of "Hellenic/Hellas" just before the nonmention of Helen's name, and after its climactic mention (868, 877–78 Greek; 886, 895–96 AS).

xiv. Hecuba here (891 Greek) plays on Helen's name and its similarity to the verb that means "take, seize, destroy." Cf. 1165 AS (1114–15 Greek) below, *Hecuba* 461 AS (443 Greek), with note, and notes xiii above and xxvii below.

xv. I omit the following line (918 Greek), which is not needed for sense and is evidently corrupt as transmitted, but probably meant something like "my own replies to match your accusations."

xvi. Because of the close repetition of two similar words meaning "justly" in these two lines (961–62 Greek), Murray, followed by Diggle and Kovacs, posited a lacuna (missing line) between them.

xvii. My translation reflects not the manuscripts' reading *hai* at 975 Greek (unless the line is delivered sarcastically), but the spirit of the text as emended by either Naber or Hartung (*ei* or *ou*, respectively), in which Hecuba questions or denies that the beauty contest on Mount Ida ever took place. With the MSS reading, Hecuba says that the goddesses did come to Mount Ida for a beauty contest, but it was just for a lark, and Hera and Athena certainly never betrayed their favorite cities by offering them as prizes. T. C. W. Stinton takes this view, and translates (*Euripides and the Judgment of Paris* [London: Society for the Promotion of Hellenic Studies, 1965], pp. 37–38):

. . . when they went to Ida
Just for amusement, out of vanity.

Parmentier translates, "C'est par badinage et par coquetterie qu'elles sont venues faire sur l'Ida leur concours de beauté." Biehl and Lee also accept the MSS reading, while Diggle, Kovacs, and Barlow prefer Hartung's *ou*. See further Michael Lloyd, "The Helen Scene in Euripides' *Troades*," *Classical Quarterly* 34 (1984): 303–13, esp. 310–11, and *The Agon in Euripides* (Oxford: Clarendon Press, 1992), pp. 105–6.

xviii. At Greek 990 Hecuba says, "And it's fitting that the goddess' name has the same beginning as *aphrosyne* [foolishness]."

xix. In this sentence I am following the text and interpretation of 1034–35 Greek outlined by Diggle 1981b, pp. 68–70, following W. R. Paton,

"Quatre Passages des *Troyennes* d'Euripide," *Revue des études grecques* 27 (1914): 35–38.

xx. Reading Ra'anana Meridor's textual emendation *katarroa,* "flowing," for the MSS' difficult *kataora,* "hanging down" ("Euripides, *Tro.* 1089–90," *Classical Quarterly* 28 [1978]: 472).

xxi. I omit the following line (1140 Greek), following Herwerden, Paley, Diggle, and Kovacs: "—this corpse's mother, Andromache, painful sight—." The line comes across as ineffective and awkward padding.

xxii. This difficult sentence (1171–72 Greek) has puzzled interpreters, and the text may be corrupt, as Diggle notes in his apparatus. Kovacs daggers 1172. John Davie translates, "But as it is, my child, you have no knowledge of seeing or discovering these pleasures in your mind; they were yours to inherit, but you had no use of them" (John N. Davie, trans., *Euripides: Electra and Other Plays* ([London: Penguin Books, 1998], p. 213).

xxiii. Reading Diggle's emendation *stego* for the manuscripts' *lego* at 1177 Greek (1981b, pp. 72–74). The Greek of the manuscripts means, "not to say disgraceful things"; Diggle emends it to mean "not to cover up disgraceful things," which better suits the preceding gruesome image.

xxiv. The manuscript tradition offers two different readings in this line (1181 Greek): *espiptôn peplous,* "falling into my robes," and *espiptôn lechos,* "falling onto my bed." Both are plausible, and modern editors are divided, with Murray and Diggle reading *peplous,* and Parmentier, Lee, Biehl, and Kovacs reading *lechos.*

xxv. The meaning is uncertain here (1211 Greek), and the text may be corrupt; Diggle daggers the phrase that I've translated as "pursue insatiably," *ouk es plêsmonas thêrômenoi,* literally, "hunting down [these pursuits] not to satiety." Lee (*ad loc.*) suggests that *es plêsmonas* means "not to excess," and that "Euripides seems to be criticising the over-emphasis which, in his opinion, his countrymen give to athletics," but this seems unlikely. Parmentier, too, translates, "ce sont jeux qu'en Phrygie on tient en honneur sans s'y adonner jusqu' à l'excès." Kovacs translates "Eden's attractive but uncertain conjecture," which gives the meaning "practices the Phrygians honor from a desire to sate the spirit of rancor."

xxvi. In the following passage, the Chorus sing and Hecuba speaks. I have italicized the sung parts.

xxvii. Playing on Astyanax's name, which means "city-lord." See further H. G. Edinger, "Euripides, 'Troades', 1217," *Hermes* 115 (1987): 378. Edinger argues that the Chorus are responding to the light play on Helen's name at 1214 Greek (*apheileth' Helenê;* 1271–72 AS), which I have tried to capture by using "withheld" in my translation. "The name Helen, they imply, was given correctly; the name Astyanax was an illusion now wrecked."

xxviii. I follow the reading of the manuscripts at 1242 Greek, *ei d'hêmâs* ("if . . . us"). However, an emendation by Stephanus has been accepted by many editors, including Diggle: *ei de mê* ("if not"). Stephanus (Henri Estienne, c. 1528–98) is the Parisian printer and classical scholar who also gave his name to the pagination of Plato's dialogues. With his reading, 1242–44 Greek would mean, "But if the divinity had not overturned things, putting what was above ground below, we would have been unknown and not have been sung of . . ." (Kovacs' translation). In Stephanus' view, a god *has* turned the world upside down; in the MSS reading, a god could have quietly obliterated Troy by burying it in the earth, with none of the epic fame that the Trojan War brought to its human participants (both heroes and victims), but this did not happen. For the idea of fame as a consolation for disaster, see Cassandra's speech at 408–12 AS. On the Trojan women's awareness of themselves as subjects of poetry, see Dana LaCourse Munteanu, "The Tragic Muse and the Anti-Epic Glory of Women in Euripides' *Troades,*" *Classical Journal* 106 (2010–11): 129–47.

xxix. My translation follows the reading and punctuation of 1288–90 Greek suggested by Sansone (1983, p. 230). The first two stanzas of this *kommos* (lyric lament) are textually problematic, and editors do not agree on whether or not they observe strophic responsion; see the following note. The meter is lyric iambics.

xxx. I omit the following two lines, 1300–1301 Greek, for the sake of preserving the strophic symmetry:

Flames, and violent spears, go raging
through the palaces.

Parmentier and Lee, however, do not mark 1287–1301 as strophic, and they retain these lines.

Suggestions for Further Reading

Editions, Commentaries, and Textual Discussions

Allen, James T., and Gabriel Italie. *A Concordance to Euripides*. Berkeley and London: University of California Press and Cambridge University Press, 1954.

Arnson Svarlien, Diane, trans. *Euripides:* Alcestis, Medea, Hippolytus. Indianapolis: Hackett, 2007.

Barlow, Shirley A., trans. and comm. *Euripides:* Trojan Women. Warminster, UK: Aris and Phillips, 1986.

Battezzato, Luigi. Review of Gregory, *Euripides:* Hecuba (1999). *Classical Journal* 96 (2000–2001): 225–26.

————, ed., trans., and comm. *Euripide,* Ecuba. Milan: Bur-Rizzoli, 2010.

————, ed. and comm. *Euripides:* Hecuba. Cambridge: Cambridge University Press, forthcoming.

Biehl, Werner, ed. *Euripides:* Troades. Leipzig: Teubner, 1970.

Borthwick, E. K. "Two Scenes of Combat in Euripides." *Journal of Hellenic Studies* 90 (1970): 15–21.

Bremer, J. M. "Euripides *Hecuba* 59–215: A Reconsideration." *Mnemosyne* 24 (1971): 232–50.

Collard, Christopher. *Supplement to the Allen and Italie Concordance to Euripides*. Gröningen: Bouma's Boekhuis N.V., 1971.

————, trans. and comm. *Euripides:* Hecuba. Warminster, UK: Aris and Phillips, 1991.

Craik, Elizabeth M. "Notes on Euripides' *Andromache*." *Classical Quarterly* 29 (1979): 62–65.

Daitz, Stephen G. *Euripides:* Hecuba. 2nd ed. Leipzig: Teubner, 1990.

Diggle, James, ed. *Euripidis Fabulae*. Vol. 2. New York: Oxford University Press, 1981a.

————. *Studies on the Text of Euripides*. Oxford: Clarendon Press, 1981b.

————, ed. *Euripidis Fabulae*. Vol. 1. New York: Oxford University Press, 1984.

————. *Euripidea.* Oxford: Clarendon Press, 1994.

Drew-Bear, Thomas. "The Trochaic Tetrameter in Greek Tragedy." *American Journal of Philology* 89 (1968): 385–405.

Garzya, Antonius. *Euripides:* Andromacha. Leipzig: Teubner, 1978.

Gregory, Justina, ed. and comm. *Euripides:* Hecuba. *Introduction, Text, and Commentary.* American Philological Association Textbook Series, 14. Atlanta: Scholars Press, 1999.

Kamerbeek, J. C. "Rereading Euripides in the New Oxford Text (Tom. I)." *Mnemosyne* 39 (1986): 92–101.

Kovacs, David. *The* Andromache *of Euripides: An Interpretation.* The American Philological Association, American Classical Studies 6. Ann Arbor, MI: Scholars Press, 1980.

————. *The Heroic Muse: Studies in the* Hippolytus *and* Hecuba *of Euripides.* AJP Monographs in Classical Philology 2. Baltimore: Johns Hopkins University Press, 1987.

————. "Coniectanea Euripidea." *Greek, Roman, and Byzantine Studies* 29, no. 2 (1988): 115–34.

————, ed. and trans. *Euripides II:* Children of Heracles, Hippolytus, Andromache, Hecuba. Cambridge, MA: Harvard University Press, 1995. Repr. with revisions and corrections, 2005.

————. *Euripidea Altera.* Mnemosyne Supplement 161. Leiden, Netherlands: Brill, 1996.

————. *Euripidea Tertia.* Mnemosyne Supplement 240. Leiden, Netherlands: Brill, 2003.

————, ed. and trans. *Euripides IV:* Trojan Women, Iphigenia among the Taurians, Ion. Cambridge, MA: Harvard University Press, 1999.

Lee, K. H., ed. and comm. *Euripides:* Troades. New York: Macmillan, 1976.

Lloyd, Michael, trans. and comm. *Euripides:* Andromache. Warminster, UK: Aris and Phillips, 1994.

Matthiessen, Kjeld. Hekabe. *Euripides.* Berlin: De Gruyter, 2008.

Méridier, Louis, ed., trans., and comm. *Euripide, Tome II.* Hippolyte, Andromaque, Hécube. 2nd ed. Paris: Les Belles Lettres, 1956.

Mueller-Goldingen, Christian. "Zu einigen Textproblemen in Euripides' Andromache." *Rheinisches Museum für Philologie* 130 (1987): 216–29.

Murray, Gilbert, ed. *Euripidis Fabulae.* Vol. 2. Oxford: Clarendon Press, 1908.

Page, Denys L. *Actors' Interpolations in Greek Tragedy.* Oxford: Clarendon Press, 1934. Repr. Garland Publishing, 1987.

Parmentier, Léon, ed., trans., and comm. *Euripide, Tome IV:* Les Troyennes, Iphigénie en Tauride, Électre. Paris: Les Belles Lettres, 1925.

Sansone, David. "Euripides, *Troades* 634–635." *Antiquité Classique* 52 (1983): 228–31.

Stevens, P. T., ed. and comm. *Euripides:* Andromache. Oxford: Clarendon Press, 1971.

Tierney, Michael. *Euripides:* Hecuba. *Edited with Introduction, Notes and Vocabulary.* Dublin: Browne and Nolan, 1946. Repr. Bristol Classical Press, 1979.

West, M. L. "Tragica IV." *Bulletin of the Institute of Classical Studies* 27 (1980): 9–22.

Willink, Charles. "Critical Notes on the 'Cantica' of Euripides' *Andromache*." *Philologus* 149, no. 2 (2005): 187–208.

Greek Tragedy

Csapo, Eric, and William J. Slater. *The Context of Ancient Drama.* Ann Arbor: University of Michigan Press, 1994.

Easterling, P. E. *The Cambridge Companion to Greek Tragedy.* Cambridge: Cambridge University Press, 1997.

Goldhill, Simon. *Reading Greek Tragedy.* Cambridge: Cambridge University Press, 1986.

Gregory, Justina, ed. *A Companion to Greek Tragedy.* Malden, MA: Blackwell, 2005.

Rabinowitz, Nancy Sorkin. *Greek Tragedy.* Malden, MA: Blackwell, 2008.

Scodel, Ruth. *An Introduction to Greek Tragedy.* New York: Cambridge University Press, 2010.

Taplin, Oliver. *Greek Tragedy in Action.* Berkeley: University of California Press, 1978.

Euripides

Arnott, Geoffrey. "Euripides and the Unexpected." *Greece and Rome* 20 (1973): 49–63.

Conacher, Desmond. *Euripides and the Sophists.* London: Duckworth, 1998.

Cropp, Martin, and Lee, Kevin, eds. *Euripides and Tragic Theatre in the Late Fifth Century.* Champaign, IL: Stipes Publishing, 2000.

de Jong, Irene J. F. *Narrative in Drama: The Art of the Euripidean Messenger-Speech*. Leiden, Netherlands: E. J. Brill, 1991.

Dunn, Francis M. *Tragedy's End: Closure and Innovation in Euripidean Drama*. New York: Oxford University Press, 1996.

Gregory, Justina. *Euripides and the Instruction of the Athenians*. Ann Arbor: University of Michigan Press, 1991.

Halleran, Michael. *Stagecraft in Euripides*. London: Croom Helm, 1985.

Mastronarde, Donald J. *The Art of Euripides: Dramatic Technique and Social Context*. Cambridge: Cambridge University Press, 2010.

Michelini, Ann. *Euripides and the Tragic Tradition*. Madison: University of Wisconsin Press, 1988.

Mossman, Judith, ed. *Oxford Readings in Classical Studies: Euripides*. Oxford: Oxford University Press, 2003.

Stinton, T. C. W. *Euripides and the Judgement of Paris*. London: Society for the Promotion of Hellenic Studies, 1965.

Winnington-Ingram, R. I. "Euripides: *Poiêtês Sophos*." *Arethusa* 2 (1969): 127–42.

Studies of *Andromache*

Allan, William. *The* Andromache *and Euripidean Tragedy*. Oxford: Oxford University Press, 2000.

Kyriakou, Poulcheria. "All in the Family: Present and Past in Euripides' 'Andromache.'" *Mnemosyne* 50 (1997): 7–26.

Mossman, Judith. "The Unity of Euripides' *Andromache*." *Greece and Rome* 43 (1996): 143–56.

Sorum, Christina E. "Euripides' Judgment: Literary Creation in *Andromache*." *American Journal of Philology* 116 (1995): 371–88.

Storey, Ian. "Domestic Disharmony in Euripides' *Andromache*." *Greece and Rome* 38 (1989): 16–27.

Studies of *Hecuba*

Kovacs, David. *The Heroic Muse: Studies in the* Hippolytus *and* Hecuba *of Euripides*. Baltimore: Johns Hopkins University Press, 1987.

Mossman, Judith. *Wild Justice: A Study of Euripides'* Hecuba. Oxford: Oxford University Press, 1995.

Scodel, Ruth. "The Captive's Dilemma: Sexual Acquiescence in Euripides' *Hecuba* and *Troades*." *Harvard Studies in Classical Philology* 98 (1998): 137–54.

Segal, Charles. "Violence and the Other: Greek, Female, and Barbarian in Euripides' Hecuba." *Transactions of the American Philological Association* 120 (1990): 109–31.

Studies of *Trojan Women*

Croally, N. T. *Euripidean Polemic:* The Trojan Women *and the Function of Tragedy*. Cambridge: Cambridge University Press, 1994.

Dyson, Michael, and K. H. Lee. "The Funeral of Astyanax in Euripides' *Troades*." *Journal of Hellenic Studies* 120 (2000): 17–33.

Meridor, Ra'anana. "Plot and Myth in Euripides' *Heracles* and *Troades*." *Phoenix* 38 (1984): 205–15.

Suter, Ann. "Lament in Euripides' *Trojan Women*." *Mnemosyne* 56 (2003): 1–28.